SMART COOKING

*Over 60 Delicious, Simple Recipes in Minutes
by Celebrity Chef Art Smith*

DEDICATON

For Grandmother Mabel Jones, who taught me how to cook in the microwave in the 1970s.
Her peanut brittle was never made on the stove top. It was always made in the microwave,
along with many delicious comforting foods for our family.

By: Chef Art Smith

Culinary Direction and Recipe Development: Sari Zernich Worsham, Leticia de Mello Bueno

Published by: Cooking Miracle, LLC

Book Design: Leslie Anne Feagley

Food Photography: Felipe Cuevas

Photography Studio: Grove Studios, Miami, Florida

Chef Art Smith Photography: Kipling Swehla Photography

Creative Direction & Food Styling: Leticia de Mello Bueno

Library of Congress Cataloging-in-Publication Data has been applied for.
ISBN 978-1-4951-9220-3

Printed in Canada

Table of Contents

Introduction 4

What is smartbowl™.................. 6

How to Use Your smartbowl™ 8

Smart Veggies 9

Eggs Your Way 10

SMARTBOWL™ RECIPES

Breakfast............................ 11

Soups and Salads 29

Side Dishes 43

Main Courses 59

Entertaining 79

Desserts 85

Pantry 97

Index 110

Introduction

From Chef Art Smith

Life is busy these days. Few of us seem to find the time to take care of ourselves. It's become difficult to take the time to cook and eat healthy, delicious food. I'm a busy professional chef and a dad of five, I know that eating well when you're busy is hard; so is preparing the family dinner. Kids are picky and managing multiple schedules is challenging. We all know what great food looks and tastes like, but how do we get that great food on our tables? Food that's not only fast and easy to prepare, but also nutritious and delicious?

My answer is smartbowl™, a revolutionary new cooking system that you can depend on for fast, consistently delicious meals that make you feel good about what you're eating. You simply can't imagine what this system can do—it will transform the way you cook and eat.

When I first started cooking with smartbowl™, I couldn't believe how little I had to do to make a delicious meal. I realized that the smartbowl™ technology does all of the work for you. This was a game-changer. Whether you want to eat healthy and watch your portions, don't know how to cook, want to experiment in the kitchen, or simply want to be able to cook delicious food in just minutes, your answer is smartbowl™.

We use technology to make our lives easier. It's time to bring technology into the kitchen to satisfy our desire for delicious food that nurtures us inside and out. In *Smart Cooking*, I've created recipes with you in mind. They will impress your family and friends. They are simple, delicious, have few ingredients, are made in minutes, and get people excited about eating well. Why not spend the extra time you'll have after cooking with smartbowl™ around the table with the ones you love?

xoxo
Art Smith

Note from the founder, Tricia Frigo

I'm a working mom of four young, hungry boys. I've always enjoyed food and cooking; the feeling of knowing I've created something delicious for my family. Going back to work changed how I felt about the family meal. It became a challenge to balance everything. I knew I needed to find a way to simplify the enormous tasks of shopping, prepping, cooking and cleaning. Then I found smartbowl™.

The smartbowl™ system transformed the way I approach the family meal; few ingredients, simple recipes, fast cooking times- no pots, pans, or casserole dishes to clean up. It's the secret weapon I rely on to make delicious, healthy meals everyone will love, in the time it used to take me to gather ingredients and pull out the pots and pans for a traditional recipe.

Chef Art created these *Smart Cooking* recipes to ensure that you can take full advantage of the smartbowl™ technology, whether you're looking to save time in the kitchen, learning how to cook or struggling to eat well. These recipes are simple, quick, easy-to-make, full of flavor—and they are on the table in less than 15 minutes. Though it may be hard to believe, each dish photographed for this book was made with the smartbowl™ system, following recipes exactly.

The smartbowl™ system is my answer to a simpler, more peaceful life. My hope is that smartbowl™ will do the same for you, helping you make time for those things that matter most.

What is smartbowl™?

Your Guide to smartbowl™ 101

The smartbowl™ system is a revolutionary new cooking system that takes the guesswork out of cooking- the cutting-edge technology does all the hard work for you. Innovative high-end materials combine to use two cooking methods simultaneously, cooking food faster and infusing moisture into the food through microwave (cooking from the inside-out) and super-saturated steam (cooking from the outside-in).

Your smartbowl™ System Components

- **The Glass Bowl** is made of state-of-the-art, ultra-thin borosilicate glass. It is temperature resistant (can go from hot to cold extremes) and has superior thermal conductivity, which provides optimal even heat quickly.

- **The Lid** is made of premium medical grade silicone, which has greater temperature and chemical durability than food grade silicone.

The smartbowl™ System

The smartbowl™ releases excess steam using two methods engineered into the lid. At low pressure, steam is released through the vent in the center of the valve. **Once maximum steam saturation has been achieved, the lid will automatically open along one edge venting excess steam, while keeping the lid in place.** This prevents overcooking, and controls moisture and temperature, ensuring even-cooking and juicy, delicious food.

What's So Smart About It?

1 *smart* dual venting system: the smartbowl™ lid vents steam in two different ways. This creates a revolutionary cooking process that infuses moisture into food and eliminates hot spots and rubbery textures common found in microwave cooking.

2 *smart* technology: The smartbowl™ system simultaneously cooks food from the inside-out (microwave) and the outside-in (super-saturated steam environment). This significantly reduces cooking time, which helps preserve vitamins and nutrients, especially those in fruits and vegetables.

The lid may open during cooking to prevent overcooking. This is a good thing! It ensures juicy, delicious, evenly-cooked food.

3 **smart lid:** The lid keeps food fresher longer in the refrigerator because it removes air when the valve is pushed down. Air is the enemy of fresh foods.

4 *smart* **life:** Be smart about the choices you make and how you spend your time. Simplify to make the time to do the things that matter most.

How to Get Started

Check your microwave's wattage!

Recipes for this book were created using a 1100- watt microwave. Every microwave is different. ***As in other cooking methods, cooking times in recipes will fluctuate slightly.*** As with any other cookbook, the cooking times suggested will serve as a guide to help you get your cookings times close to where they should be.

Always err on less cooking time. Check food and add time in small increments. Don't assume that if you double the recipe, you double the time. You can always add time, but you can't take it back!

Leaving the lid on the smartbowl™ after cooking will continue to cook your food. If a recipe says to let the smartbowl™ sit with the lid on for 5 minutes- set a timer or food can overcook.

Use your judgment and write notes on your recipes to help your cooking become more efficient.

How to Use Your smartbowl™

The smartbowl™ system is the must-have tool that helps to simply your life and your kitchen.

Meals to go: Eat your salad, or bring your lunch to microwave at work. Salmon and Kale is a simple recipe to prep ahead to bring with you (see page 65).

Simple storage: Store in your pantry, refrigerator or freezer. Press the valve to remove unwanted air.

Fast meal preparation: Most *Smart Cooking* recipes take about 10 minutes to prepare.

Easy measure: Measure directly in the smartbowl™ with convenient cup measurement markings.

One bowl convenience: Prep, cook, serve and store in one bowl. One bowl to clean up- no pots, pans or dishes to wash!

CAUTION!
Smartbowl™ Gets Really Hot!

Smartbowl™ conducts heats very well and quickly.

Always:

- Be careful when draining water and other liquids.
- Be careful when you remove the lid, the steam can be hot.
- Be mindful of the amount of liquid you pour into your smartbowl™. You need to leave room for the supersaturated steam technology to work.

Place the lid on the smartbowl™ and push down to seal it .

Push down on the valve to release the air.

Place the smartbowl™ in the microwave, oven, or on the stovetop. Remove smartbowl™ from the microwave using oven mitts.

Smart Veggies

The smartbowl™ system transforms vegetables. The texture, the color and the flavor are all very intense, due to the speed with which it cooks.

Tips from Chef Art:

- For best results, use fresh vegetables instead of frozen (you can use frozen, but fresh veggies turn out best) and room temperature water. Cold water will increase cooking times.

- The smartbowl™ system recipes suggest cooking times that produce more al dente vegetables. If you like them softer, or more well-done, add time in 20-30 second increments.

- All they need is a great extra virgin olive oil, and some salt and pepper. Delicious!

Smart Veggies	MEDIUM BOWL 1–2 Servings	Microwave Cooking Times (in minutes)	LARGE BOWL 2–4 Servings	Microwave Cooking Times (in minutes)
Before cooking, place the lid on the smartbowl™, seal it and press the valve to release air.				
beets ($1/2$" - 1" quarters)	1 cup beets, $1/2$ cup water*	3:30	2 cups beets, 1 cup water	6:00
broccoli (florets)	1 cup broccoli, $1/2$ cup water*	3:00	2 cups broccoli, 1 cup water	4:30
Brussels sprouts (whole or halved)	1 cup Brussels sprouts, $1/2$ cup water	3:00	2 cups Brussels sprouts, 1 cup water	5:30
baby carrots (whole)	1 cup carrots, $1/2$ cup water	3:30	2 cups carrots, 1 cup water	6:00
cauliflower (florets)	1 cup cauliflower, $1/2$ cup water*	3:00	2 cups cauliflower, 1 cup water	5:30
corn on the cob (broken in half)	1 cob broken in half, no water	1:30	2 cobs broken in half, no water*	2:00
green beans (cut into 3" pieces)	1 cup green beans, $1/2$ cup water*	1:30	2 cups green beans, 1 cup water	2:00
snap peas (whole)	1 cup snap peas, $1/2$ cup water	1:30	2 cups snap peas, 1 cup water	2:00
sweet potatoes ($1/2$" - 1" cubes)	1 cup sweet potato, $1/2$ cup water	3:30	2 cups sweet potato, 1 cup water *	6:00
zucchini ($1/2$" half moons)	1 cup zucchini, $1/2$ cup water	2:00	2 cups zucchini, 1 cup water	2:30

The times above are suggested for al dente veggies. If you like your veggies softer, either increase the time slightly, or allow your veggies to sit covered in the smartbowlTM for a few minutes after cooking.

Eggs Your Way, Every Day

1 FRIED EGG			
	1. Coat smartbowl™ with olive oil	2. Crack egg into smartbowl™	3. Place the lid on the smartbowl™, seal it and press the valve to release air.	3. Microwave cook time
Over Medium	¹/₂ teaspoon			40 seconds
Sunny Side Up	¹/₂ teaspoon			30 seconds

SOFT POACHED EGGS			
	1. Add water	2. Crack egg/s into smartbowl™	3. Place the lid on the smartbowl™, seal it and press the valve to release air.	4. Microwave cook time
1 Egg	¹/₂ cup			45 seconds
2 Eggs	1 ¹/₂ cup			1 minute, 45 seconds
3 Eggs	1 ¹/₂ cup			1 minute, 45 seconds

SCRAMBLED EGGS					
	1. Coat smartbowl™ with olive oil	2. Crack egg/s into smartbowl™ and stir	3. Place the lid on the smartbowl™, seal it and press the valve to release air.	4. Microwave cook time	5. Stir	6. Microwave cook time
1 Egg	¹/₂ teaspoon			15 seconds		15 seconds
2 Eggs	¹/₂ teaspoon			30 seconds		25 seconds
3 Eggs	¹/₂ teaspoon			45 seconds		35 seconds

Remember, this chart is meant to be used as a guide. Cooking times will vary, depending on your microwave and the temperature of the eggs and water. Try eggs our way first, and then adjust your time accordingly!

BREAKFAST

HUEVOS RANCHEROS, PAGE 28

SERVINGS | 1–2
PREP TIME | 1 MINUTE
COOK TIME | 2 MINUTES
USE | LARGE SMARTBOWL™

CREAMY BOURSIN® CHEESE SCRAMBLED EGGS

ingredients

½ teaspoon extra virgin olive oil

1 tablespoon milk

2 tablespoons Boursin® cheese

3 eggs

kosher salt and black pepper

directions

1 Coat the bottom of the large smartbowl™ with olive oil. Whisk in milk, Boursin cheese and eggs. Season with salt and pepper.

2 Place the lid on the smartbowl™, seal the lid, and press the valve to release air. Microwave for 1 ½ minutes.

3 Take the smartbowl™ out of the microwave and stir. Replace the lid and return to the microwave for 30 seconds. Mix and serve.

SERVINGS | 2
PREP TIME | 10 MINUTES
COOK TIME | ABOUT 5 MINUTES
USE | LARGE SMARTBOWL™

TRADITIONAL SOUTHERN HAM HASH

ingredients

$^1/_2$ **cup ham, cut into** $^1/_2$**-inch dice**

$^2/_3$ **cup peeled Yukon Gold potato, diced**

$^1/_3$ **cup diced red or green pepper**

kosher salt and black pepper

$^1/_4$ **cup grated cheddar**

1 tablespoon parsley, chopped

2 Eggs Your Way (see page 10)

directions

1   Place the ham, potatoes and peppers in the large smartbowl™. Place the lid on the smartbowl™, seal it and press the valve to release air. Microwave for 4 minutes.

2   Carefully remove the smartbowl™ from the microwave. Season with salt and pepper and fold in the cheddar and parsley. Split the hash onto 2 serving dishes and top each with an egg.

SERVINGS | 4
PREP TIME | 5 MINUTES
COOK TIME | ABOUT 5 MINUTES
USE | SMALL AND LARGE SMARTBOWL™

FRENCH TOAST BREAD PUDDING

ingredients

2 tablespoons butter

2 to 3 slices of challah bread, cubed

3 eggs

4 tablespoons sugar

$^1/_2$ cup milk

$^1/_8$ cup half and half

cinnamon, to taste

maple syrup, to taste

powdered sugar, to taste

directions

1   Set oven to broil.

2   Place butter in the small smartbowl™. Place the lid on the smartbowl™, seal the lid, and press the valve to release air. Microwave for 20 seconds.

3   Arrange challah bread in the large smartbowl™. Pour the melted butter over the bread and toss gently until bread is coated.

4   In a mixing bowl, combine eggs, sugar, milk, half and half and cinnamon. Pour over the buttered challah bread in the large smartbowl™ and toss to coat. Place the lid on the smartbowl™, seal the lid, and press the valve to release air. Microwave for 1 minute.

5   Carefully remove the smartbowl™ from the microwave and mix ingredients well. Place the lid on the smartbowl™, seal the lid, and press the valve to release air. Return the smartbowl™ to the microwave and cook for an additional 1 $^1/_2$ minutes.

6   Remove the smartbowl™ from the microwave and let stand for 2 minutes covered.

7   Remove the lid of the smartbowl™. Place smartbowl™ under the broiler for about 2 to 3 minutes, until the top of the pudding is golden brown.

8   Drizzle with maple syrup and sprinkle with powdered sugar.

SERVINGS | 1
PREP TIME | 5 MINUTES
COOK TIME | ABOUT 1 MINUTE
USE | LARGE SMARTBOWL™

MEDITERRANEAN POACHED EGG

ingredients

¹/₂ cup canned crushed tomatoes

¹/₈ teaspoon ground cumin

1 teaspoon chopped garlic

¹/₈ teaspoon smoked paprika

¹/₈ teaspoon cayenne pepper

kosher salt and black pepper

1 extra large egg

1 teaspoon extra virgin olive oil

1 teaspoon chopped fresh parsley

1 teaspoon chopped fresh cilantro

1 tablespoon feta cheese

directions

1   Combine the tomatoes, cumin, garlic, paprika, and cayenne in the large smartbowl™ and season with salt and pepper.

2   Crack the egg over the tomato mixture, place the lid on the smartbowl™, seal it and press the valve to release air. Microwave for 1 minute until the egg is soft poached. Add time in 15 second intervals, depending on how you like your egg.

3   Top with the olive oil, chopped parsley and cilantro, and feta cheese.

SERVINGS | 4
PREP TIME | 10 MINUTES
COOK TIME | ABOUT 15 MINUTES
USE | SMALL, MEDIUM AND LARGE SMARTBOWL™

CARAMELIZED ONION, SPINACH & GRUYERE STRATA

ingredients

1 tablespoons butter

3 cups day-old baguette bread, cut into 1" cubes

2 extra large eggs, lightly beaten

$^1/_2$ cup whole milk

pinch of nutmeg

1 cup shredded Gruyere cheese

Caramelized Onions (see page 100)

$^1/_2$ cup packed spinach, chopped

kosher salt and black pepper

directions

1 Set oven to broil.

2 To make the strata: place butter into the small smartbowl™. Place the lid on the smartbowl™, seal the lid, and press the valve to release air. Microwave for 20 seconds.

3 Place the baguette cubes in the large smartbowl™. Pour the melted butter over the baguette cubes and toss gently until the cubes are covered in butter. Set aside.

4 In a separate bowl, whisk together the eggs, milk, nutmeg, half of the Gruyere cheese and season with salt and pepper. Pour this mixture over the bread that was set aside in the large smartbowl™. Fold in caramelized onions and spinach.

5 Place the lid on the large smartbowl™ containing the cheese and bread, seal the lid, and press the valve to release air. Microwave for 3 minutes. Take smartbowl™ out of the microwave, remove the lid, and mix contents.

6 Add the other half of the Gruyere cheese to the contents of the smartbowl™. Place the lid on the smartbowl™, seal the lid, and press the valve to release air. Microwave for another 1 $^1/_2$ minutes.

7 Remove lid and place the smartbowl™ under the broiler on a rack in the middle of the oven for 4 to 5 minutes, until crisp and golden brown.

SERVINGS | 2
PREP TIME | 10 MINUTES
COOK TIME | ABOUT 5 MINUTES
USE | MEDIUM AND LARGE SMARTBOWL™

TURKEY SAUSAGE STUFFED PEARS

ingredients

1 tablespoon lemon juice, mixed with a little water

1 large pear, cut in half lengthwise with core scooped out, seeded and chopped (reserve)

2 teaspoons extra virgin olive oil

¼ pound ground turkey

1 garlic clove, minced

½ shallot, chopped

1 teaspoon parsley, chopped

1 teaspoon sage, chopped

1 teaspoon rosemary, chopped

¼ teaspoon cumin

kosher salt and black pepper

pinch of red pepper flakes, to taste

1 tablespoon chopped almonds or hazelnuts

Egg Your Way—optional (see page 10)

directions

1   In a dish, add lemon juice and water. Dip each pear, cut side down in the water and lemon mixture to prevent pear from turning brown.

2   Put olive oil, turkey, garlic, shallot and seeded core of the pear into the medium smartbowl™. Place the lid on the smartbowl™, seal the lid, and press valve to release air. Microwave for 1 ½ minutes.

3   Remove the smartbowl™ from the microwave and break up the turkey with a fork. Add herbs and spices, salt and both peppers. Place the lid on the smartbowl™, seal the lid, and press valve to release air. Microwave for another minute, or until turkey is fully cooked. Remove smartbowl™ from the microwave.

4   Place pears in the large smartbowl™. Carefully spoon the turkey mixture into the cavity of each pear half. Place the lid on the smartbowl™, seal the lid, and press valve to release air. Microwave for 2 minutes, or until pears are soft. Add chopped nuts.

TIP: You can add an Egg Your Way to the top of your stuffed pear.

SERVINGS | 4
PREP TIME | 10 MINUTES PLUS OVERNIGHT STORAGE
COOK TIME | ABOUT 1 TO 2 MINUTES
USE | LARGE SMARTBOWL™

OVERNIGHT BANANA-PECAN OATMEAL

ingredients

$1/2$ cup toasted pecans, chopped

2 cups rolled oats

1 can coconut milk (about 13 $1/2$ ounces)

2 to 4 tablespoons water (optional)

1 tablespoon ground cinnamon

1 large banana, sliced

honey or maple syrup

directions

1   Preheat oven to 375°F.

2   Place pecans on a baking sheet and toast for about 5 to 7 minutes, until fragrant. Allow pecans to cool. Store in an airtight container overnight.

3   Place oats and cinnamon in the large smartbowl™. Cover with the lid and shake. Remove the lid and pour in coconut milk. Add water if a thinner consistency is desired. Fold in bananas. Place the lid on the smartbowl™, seal the lid, and press valve to release air. Refrigerate overnight.

4   In the morning, remove the smartbowl™ with the oatmeal from the refrigerator and microwave for 1 to $1/2$ minutes.

5   Sprinkle with toasted pecans. Add honey or syrup. May be served warm from the microwave or at room temperature.

SERVINGS | 4
PREP TIME | 5 MINUTES
COOK TIME | ABOUT 2 MINUTES
USE | LARGE SMARTBOWL™

HOMEMADE BLUEBERRY JAM

ingredients

1 cup fresh blueberries

$1/4$ cup sugar

$1/2$ teaspoon powdered pectin

a pinch of cinnamon

$1/2$ lemon, juiced

toast

lemon zest

directions

1 Put the blueberries, sugar, pectin, cinnamon and lemon juice in the large smartbowl™. Place the lid on the smartbowl™, seal it and press the valve to release air. Microwave for 2 minutes. Stir and refrigerate, covered, until set.

2 Serve on toast and sprinkle with the lemon zest.

SERVINGS | 2
PREP TIME | 5 MINUTES
COOK TIME | ABOUT 5 MINUTES
USE | LARGE SMARTBOWL™

BLEU CHEESE OMELETTE WITH BACON

ingredients

2 strips of bacon, thick cut

4 extra large eggs

kosher salt and black pepper

$1/4$ cup bleu cheese, crumbled

chives, chopped

directions

1 Place 1 strip of bacon in a ring along the inside of the large smartbowl™, fatty side up. Microwave for $1^1/_2$ minutes without the lid for a crispy consistency. Remove bacon from the smartbowl™ with tongs, and place on a plate lined with a paper towel. Repeat with second strip of bacon. Drain, crumble bacon and set aside.

2 Beat 4 eggs in the same large smartbowl™ where you cooked the bacon. No need to wash. Season with salt and pepper. Place the lid on the smartbowl™, seal the lid, and press valve to release air. Microwave for 1 minute. Remove from the microwave and stir.

3 Add bleu cheese to the egg mixture and stir again. Microwave for 1 minute. Remove the smartbowl™ from the microwave and stir again.

4 Place the lid back on the smartbowl™, seal the lid and press value to release air. Microwave for 30 seconds. Remove from the microwave and stir again. Let sit covered for 2 minutes.

5 Sprinkle with crumbled bacon and chives.

SERVINGS | 1
PREP TIME | 2 MINUTES
COOK TIME | 1 MINUTE
USE | MEDIUM SMARTBOWL™

CHEF ART'S SMART START BLUEBERRY OATMEAL

ingredients

$^1/_2$ **cup quick-cooking or old-fashioned oats**

$^3/_4$ **cup water**

$^1/_2$ **tablespoon chia seeds**

$^1/_4$ **teaspoon ground cinnamon**

$^1/_3$ **cup fresh blueberries**

1 tablespoon walnuts, toasted if you like

drizzle of grade A or B maple syrup

directions

1 Combine oats, water and chia seeds in the medium smartbowl™. Place the lid on the smartbowl™, seal the lid, and press the valve to release air. Microwave for 1 minute.

2 Carefully remove from the microwave. Let the smartbowl™ sit, covered for 1 minute.

3 Add cinnamon, berries and walnuts. Drizzle with syrup.

SERVINGS | 1
PREP TIME | 5 MINUTES
COOK TIME | ABOUT 1 MINUTE
USE | MEDIUM SMARTBOWL™

HUEVOS RANCHEROS

ingredients

$^1/_2$ **cup water**

1 large egg

1 tortilla, heated

kosher salt and black pepper

2 tablespoons store-bought salsa

2 tablespoons grated pepper jack or cheddar cheese

1 teaspoon scallions, sliced

1 teaspoon cilantro, chopped

optional: sour cream and sliced avocado

directions

1   Pour $^1/_2$ cup of water into the medium smartbowl™ (make sure to use the appropriate amount of water). Break egg into the water and place the lid on. Seal the lid and press the valve to release air. Microwave for 45 seconds. Check for desired doneness. Add time if needed in 10- to 15-second intervals. Drain egg gently on a paper towel.

2   Warm tortilla: place the tortilla in the large smartbowl™. Microwave uncovered for 15 seconds.

3   Place egg on top of the warm tortilla and season with salt and pepper. Spoon salsa over egg. Sprinkle cheese, scallions and cilantro on top. Serve immediately with sour cream and sliced avocado, if desired.

TIP: If you prefer your egg another way, see the Eggs Your Way chart on page 10.

SOUPS AND SALADS

SERVINGS | 1
PREP TIME | 10 MINUTES
USE | LARGE SMARTBOWL™

FARMHOUSE CHOPPED SALAD TO-GO

ingredients

¹/₄ **cup beets, peeled and shredded**

¹/₄ **cup carrots, shredded**

¹/₂ **cup red cabbage, shredded**

¹/₂ **cup yellow bell peppers, julienned**

1 ¹/₂ **cups spinach**

¹/₄ **cup cooked quinoa**

2 tablespoons sunflower seeds, toasted

2 tablespoons Green Goddess Dressing (see page 101)

4 ounces Weeknight Chicken-see page 78 (use Dijon Mustard Marinade—see page 105)

directions

1 Add all ingredients except salad dressing into the large smartbowl™. Place the lid on the smartbowl™, seal it, and take the smartbowl™ wherever you're going. Keep refrigerated until ready to eat.

2 When ready to serve, pour Green Goddess dressing over the salad. Place the lid on the smartbowl™ and shake. Add chicken, if desired.

SERVINGS | 1–2
PREP TIME | 10 MINUTES
USE | LARGE SMARTBOWL™

BEET & ORANGE SALAD TO-GO

ingredients

¹/₂ cup Cooked Pickled Beets (see page 99)

2 cups arugula

1 orange, peeled and segmented

¹/₄ cup fennel or red onion, sliced paper-thin

2 tablespoons goat cheese

¹/₄ cup walnuts, toasted and chopped

kosher salt and black pepper

2 tablespoons Orange Vinaigrette (see page 103)

directions

1   Remove beets from pickling liquid.

2   Place arugula, orange segments, fennel, goat cheese, and walnuts in the large smartbowl™. Top with beets. Place the lid on the smartbowl™ and seal it. Take the smartbowl™ wherever you're going or serve immediately. Keep refrigerated until ready to eat.

3   When ready to serve, drizzle with Orange Vinaigrette and season to taste with salt and pepper. Place the lid on the smartbowl™, seal, shake and serve.

SERVINGS | 1
PREP TIME | 10 MINUTES
USE | LARGE SMARTBOWL™

MEDITERRANEAN SALAD TO-GO

ingredients

2 cups salad greens, loosely packed

$^1/_2$ cup tabbouleh (see page 45)

$^1/_3$ cup canned chickpeas, drained and rinsed

2 tablespoons sundried tomatoes, chopped

1 tablespoon pine nuts, toasted

1 tablespoons pitted Kalamata olives, chopped

2 tablespoons Feta cheese, crumbled

kosher salt and black pepper

1 $^1/_2$ tablespoons Mediterranean Salad Dressing (see page 102)

directions

1 Place all ingredients except salad dressing in the large smartbowl™. Place the lid on the smartbowl™, seal it, and take the smartbowl™ wherever you're going. Keep refrigerated until ready to eat.

2 When ready to serve, pour Mediterranean Salad Dressing over the salad. Place the lid on the smartbowl™ and shake.

SERVINGS | 2–4
PREP TIME | 10 MINUTES
COOK TIME | ABOUT 5 MINUTES
USE | LARGE SMARTBOWL™

RESTORATIVE VEGETABLE MISO SOUP

ingredients

1 teaspoon sesame oil

$^1/_2$ cup onions, chopped

$^1/_2$ cup butternut squash, peeled and in $^1/_2$-inch cubes

1 cup mushrooms, cleaned and sliced

1 tablespoon white miso paste

1 $^1/_2$ tablespoons Asian Marinade (see page 105)

1 cup water

1 cup low-sodium vegetable broth

4 cups spinach leaves, loosely packed

1 cup bok choy, chopped

red pepper flakes or hot sauce, to taste

kosher salt and white pepper

fresh cilantro, chopped

2 tablespoons scallions, chopped

2 teaspoons sesame seeds, toasted

1 lime, quartered

directions

1 Place sesame oil, onions and squash in the large smartbowl™. Place the lid over the bowl, seal and press the valve to release air. Microwave for 1 minute.

2 Remove the smartbowl™ from the microwave and add mushrooms, miso paste, Asian Marinade and water. Place the lid on the smartbowl™, seal the lid, and press valve to release air. Microwave for 2 minutes.

3 Carefully remove the smartbowl™ from the microwave and add vegetable broth, spinach and bok choy. Place the lid on the smartbowl™, seal the lid, and press valve to release air. Microwave for 3 minutes.

4 Remove smartbowl™ from the microwave. Allow soup to stand in the smartbowl™ with the lid on for 5 minutes while it continues to cook.

5 To serve: Ladle soup into bowls and season with red pepper flakes, salt and pepper. Sprinkle with cilantro, scallions and sesame seeds. Squeeze lime juice into the soup.

SERVINGS | 2–4
PREP TIME | 15 MINUTES
COOK TIME | ABOUT 6 MINUTES
USE | LARGE SMARTBOWL™

CAULIFLOWER, LEEK, & FENNEL SOUP

ingredients

1 tablespoon extra virgin olive oil

¹/₄ cup leeks, cleaned, chopped (white part only)

¹/₄ cup fennel, chopped (white part only, save the fronds)

¹/₄ cup pear, peeled and chopped

1 cup cauliflower, peeled, cored and chopped

2 cups low-sodium vegetable broth, divided

kosher sea salt and white pepper to taste

2 tablespoons fennel fronds, chopped

directions

1   Place olive oil, leeks, fennel, and pear in the large smartbowl™. Place the lid on the smartbowl™, seal the lid, and press the valve to release air. Microwave for 30 seconds.

2   Remove the smartbowl™ from the microwave and add the cauliflower and 1 cup of broth. Place the lid on the smartbowl™, seal the lid, and press the valve to release air. Microwave for 3 minutes.

3   Carefully remove the smartbowl™ from the microwave and add the other cup of vegetable broth. Season with salt and white pepper. Place the lid on the smartbowl™, seal the lid, and press the valve to release air. Microwave for an additional 3 minutes, or until cauliflower is tender.

4   Remove the smartbowl™ from the microwave. Allow ingredients to continue cooking in the smartbowl™ with the lid on for 2 minutes.

5   Using an immersion blender, blend soup until desired consistency is achieved. Adjust seasonings. Serve immediately in small soup cups garnished with fennel fronds.

SERVINGS | 2–4
PREP TIME | 10 MINUTES
COOK TIME | ABOUT 6 MINUTES
USE | LARGE SMARTBOWL™

CREAMY BUTTERNUT SQUASH & APPLE SOUP

ingredients

2 cups of butternut squash, peeled and cubed

1 small apple, peeled and chopped

1 cup of low-sodium vegetable stock

3 tablespoons heavy cream

3 tablespoons maple syrup

kosher salt and black pepper

Optional: 3 marshmallows

directions

1   Place butternut squash and the chopped apple in the large smartbowl™. Add the stock. Place the lid on, push down to seal and press the valve to release air. Microwave for 3 minutes. Stir and microwave for 3 more minutes. Test squash for doneness. Add time, if necessary, in 1-minute intervals, until cooked.

2   Using an immersion blender, blend until smooth. Add the cream and the maple syrup, to taste. Season with salt and pepper.

OPTIONAL: Place 3 marshmallows on top of the soup and place under the broiler for 2 minutes, until golden brown.

SERVINGS | 2
PREP TIME | 5 MINUTES
COOK TIME | ABOUT 5 MINUTES
USE | LARGE SMARTBOWL™

TUSCAN TOMATO SOUP

ingredients

¹/₄ onion, finely chopped

2 cloves of garlic, chopped

1 teaspoon extra virgin olive oil

2 cups canned crushed tomatoes

cayenne pepper

2 teaspoons sugar

¹/₂ cup of stale Italian bread, cut into 1" cubes

1 tablespoon chopped fresh basil

kosher salt and black pepper

directions

1   Place the onion and garlic in the large smartbowl™. Drizzle with olive oil. Place the lid on the smartbowl™, seal it and press the valve to release air. Microwave for 2 minutes to soften.

2   Carefully remove from the microwave. Add crushed tomatoes and place the lid back on, push to seal and press valve to release air. Microwave for 2 minutes. Stir and cook for 1 more minute.

3   Remove the smartbowl™ from the microwave and stir, adding a dusting of cayenne pepper and sugar. Stir and add ¹/₂ cup of Italian bread. Place the lid back on and let it sit for 3 to 5 minutes. Add more cubed bread for thicker soup.

4   Season with salt and pepper. Sprinkle with fresh basil and drizzle with olive oil.

SERVINGS | 4
PREP TIME | 10 MINUTES
COOK TIME | ABOUT 6 MINUTES
USE | LARGE SMARTBOWL™

PEA & SUMMER SQUASH SOUP

ingredients

3 tablespoons extra virgin olive oil, divided

2 cloves garlic, chopped

$^1/_2$ medium onion, chopped

1 cup summer squash, chopped

1 cup frozen peas, thawed

$^1/_2$ cup water, divided

$^1/_2$ cup low-sodium vegetable stock

1 cup spinach leaves

1 tablespoon fresh lemon juice,

$^1/_3$ cup basil or mint leaves

$^1/_4$ cup Greek yogurt

lemon zest from $^1/_2$ lemon, to taste

kosher salt and black pepper

directions

1 Place 1 tablespoon olive oil, garlic, onion and squash in the large smartbowl™. Place the lid on the smartbowl™, seal the lid, and press valve to release air. Microwave for about $1^1/_2$ to 2 minutes, until the onions are translucent. Set aside.

2 Stir the peas into the onion mix, along with $^1/_4$ cup of water. Place the lid on the smartbowl™, seal the lid, and press valve to release air. Microwave for about 2 minutes.

3 Pour the stock and remaining water into the smartbowl™. Place the lid on the smartbowl™, seal the lid, and press valve to release air. Microwave for about 2 minutes.

4 Pour the squash and pea soup into a blender. Blend until smooth, add spinach, lemon juice, 1 tablespoon of olive oil, and basil leaves and blend again, until desired smoothness.

5 Whisk in Greek yogurt and lemon zest. Pour into serving bowls, drizzle remaining olive oil, and season with salt and pepper. Serve warm or cold.

SERVINGS | 1–2
PREP TIME | 10 MINUTES
COOK TIME | ABOUT 4 MINUTES
USE | LARGE SMARTBOWL™

TURKEY CHILI

ingredients

1 teaspoon extra virgin olive oil

3 tablespoons sweet onion, chopped

¼ cup ground turkey

¼ teaspoon Mexican Spiced Chocolate Blend , (see page 94—optional)

1 teaspoon chili powder

½ teaspoon ground cumin

¼ teaspoon chipotle powder

⅓ cup San Marzano tomatoes, diced

⅓ cup tomato sauce

1 can red kidney beans (12 ounces), strained and rinsed

½ cup cheddar cheese

¼ cup Greek yogurt

¼ cup scallions, chopped

¼ cup avocado, diced

kosher salt and black pepper

directions

1 Place olive oil, onion, and turkey in the large smartbowl™. Place the lid on the smartbowl™, seal the lid, and press valve to release air. Microwave for 1 minute.

2 Remove the lid and crumble the turkey with a fork. Add the Mexican Spiced Chocolate Blend, chili powder, cumin, chipotle powder, tomatoes, tomato sauce and beans. Place the lid on the smartbowl™, seal the lid, and press valve to release air. Microwave for 3 minutes.

3 Carefully remove the smartbowl™ from the microwave. Allow the chili to sit in the smartbowl™ with the lid on for 1 minute while it continues to cook.

4 After 1 minute, stir and season with salt and pepper. Top with cheese, yogurt, scallions and avocado.

SIDE DISHES

MUSHROOM RAGOUT, PAGE 56

SERVINGS | 2
PREP TIME | 10 MINUTES
COOK TIME | ABOUT 6 $^1/_2$ MINUTES PLUS 30 MINUTES TO CHILL
USE | MEDIUM AND LARGE SMARTBOWL™

TABBOULEH

ingredients

1 cup water or low-sodium vegetable stock, hot

6 tablespoons bulgur or cracked wheat

pinch of pumpkin spice

$^2/_3$ cup tomatoes, chopped and seeded

$^1/_4$ cup flat leaf parsley, chopped

$^1/_4$ cup mint, chopped

2 tablespoons extra virgin olive oil

$^1/_2$ lemon, juiced

3 scallions, chopped

kosher salt and black pepper

directions

1 Pour $^1/_2$ cup hot water or stock into the medium smartbowl™. Place the lid on the smartbowl™, seal the lid, and press valve to release air. Microwave for 1 $^1/_2$ minutes.

2 Carefully remove smartbowl™ from the microwave. Place bulgur and pumpkin spice in the large smartbowl™. Pour in boiling liquid. Place the lid on the smartbowl™, seal the lid, and press valve to release air. Let stand until cool, approximately 5 minutes.

3 Mix tomatoes, parsley, mint, olive oil, lemon juice, and scallions into the bulgur. Season with salt and pepper.

4 Cover and refrigerate for at least 30 minutes.

SERVINGS | 4
PREP TIME | 8 MINUTES
COOK TIME | ABOUT 2 $\frac{1}{2}$ MINUTES
USE | LARGE SMARTBOWL™

MOROCCAN COUSCOUS

ingredients

$\frac{1}{2}$ **cup sweet onion, chopped**

1 clove garlic, crushed

1 teaspoon Moroccan Spice Blend (see page 107)

1 $\frac{3}{4}$ cups low-sodium chicken or vegetable broth

1 cup couscous

6-8 dried apricots, chopped

$\frac{1}{4}$ **cup toasted almonds, sliced or chopped**

1 teaspoon orange zest

kosher salt and black pepper

directions

1 Place onions, crushed garlic, spice blend, broth, and couscous in the large smartbowl™. Place the lid on the smartbowl™, seal the lid, and press the valve to release air. Microwave for 2 $\frac{1}{2}$ minutes.

2 Carefully remove the smartbowl™ from the microwave and set aside for 6 minutes with the lid on. Test for doneness.

3 When couscous is cooked completely, fluff with a fork and add apricots, almonds, orange zest, salt and pepper to taste.

SERVINGS | 2
PREP TIME | 5 MINUTES
COOK TIME | ABOUT 6 MINUTES
USE | LARGE SMARTBOWL™

GINGER-SOY BRUSSELS SPROUTS

ingredients

2 cups Brussels sprouts

1 cup water

¹/₃ cup cup Asian Marinade (see page 105)

1 tablespoon brown sugar

directions

1   Place an oven rack in the upper half of your oven, but not too close to the broiler. Set your oven to broil.

2   Put Brussels sprouts into the large smartbowl™ and add water. Place the lid on the smartbowl™, seal the lid, and press the valve to release air. Microwave for 3 to 4 minutes, adding time in 30-second intervals to reach desired doneness.

3   Remove smartbowl™ from microwave and carefully strain water using a strainer or the lid. Be careful—water will be very hot!

4   Pour Asian Marinade and sugar into the smartbowl™ with the Brussels sprouts. Place the lid on, seal it and shake to mix. Place in the oven, uncovered, for 4 to 5 minutes or until sauce has caramelized.

SERVINGS | 4
PREP TIME | 10 MINUTES
COOK TIME | ABOUT 4 MINUTES
USE | MEDIUM AND LARGE SMARTBOWL™

BRAISED KALE WITH LARDONS

ingredients

$1/3$ **cup bacon lardons cut into 1-inch matchsticks (or 2 slices hickory smoked bacon, chopped)**

1 garlic clove, sliced

1 shallot, chopped

2 teaspoons extra virgin olive oil

12 kale leaves, torn by hand; ribs chopped into $1/8$-inch rounds

3 tablespoons low-sodium vegetable stock

kosher salt and black pepper

directions

1 Place lardons or chopped bacon in the medium smartbowl™. Cook in the microwave, uncovered, for 1 to $1/2$ minutes.

2 Remove the lardons/bacon from the smartbowl™ and drain on a plate lined with a paper towel. Let cool.

3 Place garlic, shallots, and olive oil in the large smartbowl™. Microwave uncovered for 30 seconds.

4 Remove the smartbowl™ from the microwave and add kale, lardons/bacon and stock. Place the lid on the smartbowl™, seal the lid, and press the valve to release air. Microwave for 2 minutes.

5 Carefully remove the smartbowl™ from the microwave, season to taste with salt and pepper, stir, and serve. Save the rendered bacon fat for a rainy day.

TIP: To cook strips of bacon in the smartbowl™, place a single strip of bacon around the sides of the medium smartbowl™, fattier side up. Microwave uncovered, for 1 to $1/2$ minutes, or until done.

SERVINGS | 2
PREP TIME | 5 MINUTES
COOK TIME | ABOUT 1 $^{1}/_{2}$ MINUTES
USE | LARGE SMARTBOWL™

GREEN BEANS ALMONDINE

ingredients

1 cup green beans

$^{1}/_{2}$ cup water

kosher salt and black pepper

1 tablespoon extra virgin olive oil

juice from $^{1}/_{2}$ lemon

$^{1}/_{4}$ cup almonds, sliced or chopped

directions

1   Place green beans in the large smartbowl™. Cover the beans with water and place the lid on, push down to seal and press the valve to release air. Microwave for 1 $^{1}/_{2}$ minutes until al dente.

2   Test for doneness, adding time in 30 second intervals if needed. Drain water and season with salt and pepper, olive oil, lemon juice and almonds.

SERVINGS | 4
PREP TIME | 5 MINUTES
COOK TIME | ABOUT 3 MINUTES
USE | SMALL SMARTBOWL™

BROCCOLI WITH THAI PEANUT SAUCE

ingredients

For the peanut sauce:

1 tablespoon ginger, grated

1 teaspoon garlic, grated

½ teaspoon local honey or sweetener of your choice

¼ cup creamy peanut butter

1 tablespoon Tamari or low-sodium soy sauce

½ tablespoon lime juice

2 tablespoons low-sodium vegetable stock

red pepper flakes to taste

For the broccoli:

2 cups broccoli florets

water

kosher salt and black pepper

directions

1 Add grated ginger and garlic to the small smartbowl™. Stir in the remaining ingredients for the sauce, mixing well.

2 Place the lid on the smartbowl™, seal the lid, and press the valve to release air. Use as desired.

3 Put broccoli into the large smartbowl™ and add water up to the 1½-cup mark on the smartbowl™. Place the lid on the smartbowl™, seal the lid, and press the valve to release air. Microwave for 3 minutes.

4 Remove the smartbowl™ from microwave and carefully strain water using a strainer or the lid. Be careful—water will be very hot!

5 Add peanut sauce and season with salt and pepper.

SERVINGS | 4
PREP TIME | 7 MINUTES
COOK TIME | ABOUT 2 MINUTES
USE | LARGE SMARTBOWL™

WARM SUMMER SQUASH WITH FETA CHEESE

ingredients

1 tablespoon extra virgin olive oil

2 cloves garlic, sliced

$1/2$ cup yellow summer squash, cut into $1/2$-inch thick half-moons

$1/2$ cup zucchini, cut into $1/2$-inch thick half-moons

2 tablespoons water

3 sprigs fresh thyme or rosemary, stemmed and chopped

2 tablespoons Kalamata olives, pitted and chopped

$1/2$ cup crumbled feta cheese

kosher salt and black pepper

directions

1 Place olive oil and garlic in the large smartbowl™. Microwave 30 seconds uncovered.

2 Add summer squash and zucchini to the olive oil and garlic. Stir. Add water. Place the lid on the smartbowl™, seal the lid, and press the valve to release air. Microwave for about $1 1/2$ minutes.

3 Remove the smartbowl™ from the microwave. Stir and season with salt and pepper. Sprinkle with herbs, olives and feta cheese. Serve warm or refrigerate.

SERVINGS | 4
PREP TIME | 5 MINUTES
COOK TIME | ABOUT 5 MINUTES
USE | LARGE SMARTBOWL™

CHEF ART'S GARLICKY MASHED CAULIFLOWER

ingredients

2 cups cauliflower, chopped

1 cup low-sodium vegetable stock

2 tablespoons grated Parmesan cheese

1 tablespoon extra virgin olive oil

1 clove of garlic, smashed and chopped

1 tablespoon Greek yogurt

kosher salt and black pepper

directions

1 Place cauliflower into the large smartbowl™. Add stock. Place the lid on the smartbowl™, seal the lid, and press the valve to release air. Microwave for about 5 minutes.

2 Carefully remove from the microwave. Let stand for 3 minutes with lid on, or until cauliflower is tender. Drain liquid and save.

3 Using an immersion blender, blend the cooked cauliflower, the cheese, olive oil, and garlic and add the broth in 1 tablespoon intervals until desired consistency. Puree until smooth. Fold in the yogurt. Season with salt and pepper.

SERVINGS | 2–4
PREP TIME | 5 MINUTES
COOK TIME | ABOUT 3 MINUTES
USE | LARGE SMARTBOWL™

CREAMY POLENTA

ingredients

¹/₃ cup instant polenta

1 cup water

¹/₃ cup milk

pinch of salt

2 tablespoons grated parmesan cheese

kosher salt and black pepper

directions

1 Pour the polenta, water and milk in the large smartbowl™ and whisk together. Place the lid on, push down to seal and press the valve to release air. Microwave for 1 minute, stir. Microwave for another minute, stir. Microwave for one last minute.

2 Carefully remove the smartbowl™ from the microwave. Season with salt and pepper and add the grated cheese. Use immediately.

SERVINGS | 4
PREP TIME | 10 MINUTES
COOK TIME | ABOUT 1 MINUTE
USE | MEDIUM SMARTBOWL™

MUSHROOM RAGOUT

ingredients

1 pound seasonal wild mushrooms, cleaned

1 tablespoon extra virgin olive oil

1 clove garlic, chopped

1 teaspoon Mediterranean Herb Blend (see page 107)

1 shallot, chopped

1 tablespoon Marsala or other wine of choice

3 tablespoons flat leaf parsley, chopped

kosher salt and black pepper

directions

1   Cut the edges of the stems off the mushrooms. Cut mushrooms in quarters or in $1/2$-inch slices.

2   Put olive oil, garlic, and herbs into the medium smartbowl™. Place the lid on the smartbowl™, seal the lid, and press the valve to release air. Microwave for 30 seconds.

3   Remove the lid from the smartbowl™. Add mushrooms, shallots, and wine. Place the lid on the smartbowl™, seal the lid, and press the valve to release air. Microwave for 30 seconds.

4   Remove the smartbowl™ from the microwave. Let stand with the lid on for 5 minutes. After 5 minutes, remove lid, sprinkle with parsley and season with salt and pepper.

SERVINGS | 2
PREP TIME | 5 MINUTES
COOK TIME | ABOUT 3 MINUTES
USE | LARGE SMARTBOWL™

SWEET POTATOES WITH MAPLE SYRUP, MARSHMALLOWS & ROSEMARY

ingredients

1 cup sweet potato, peeled, medium dice

1 tablespoon maple syrup

1 sprig rosemary

1 teaspoon extra virgin olive oil

kosher salt and black pepper

¹/₂ cup mini marshmallows

directions

1 Preheat oven to broil .

2 Combine the sweet potato, maple syrup, rosemary, and olive oil in the large smartbowl™, and season with salt and pepper. Place the lid on, push down to seal and press the valve to release air. Microwave for 3 minutes, or until sweet potatoes are soft.

3 Carefully remove the smartbowl™ from the microwave. Remove rosemary and top sweet potatoes with marshmallows. Place the lid on, push down to seal and press the valve to release air. Microwave for 30 seconds. Remove from the microwave and remove lid. Pop under the broiler for 30 seconds until golden brown. Serve warm.

SERVINGS | 2
PREP TIME | 6 MINUTES
COOK TIME | ABOUT 3 $\frac{1}{2}$ MINUTES
USE | LARGE SMARTBOWL™

FINGERLING POTATOES

ingredients

6 small fingerling potatoes

1 $\frac{1}{2}$ cups water

$\frac{1}{2}$ tablespoon extra virgin olive oil

kosher salt and black pepper

directions

1   Place potatoes in the large smartbowl™ and fill with water. Place the lid on the smartbowl™, seal the lid, and press valve to release air. Microwave for 3 $\frac{1}{2}$ minutes.

2   Check potatoes to see if they are done. Add additional cooking time in 30 second intervals if needed. Strain potatoes when cooked thoroughly.

3   Drizzle with extra virgin olive oil. Season with salt and pepper. Place the lid on the smartbowl™, seal it, and shake the contents. Remove lid and serve.

MAIN COURSES

LINGUINE & MUSSELS, PAGE 72

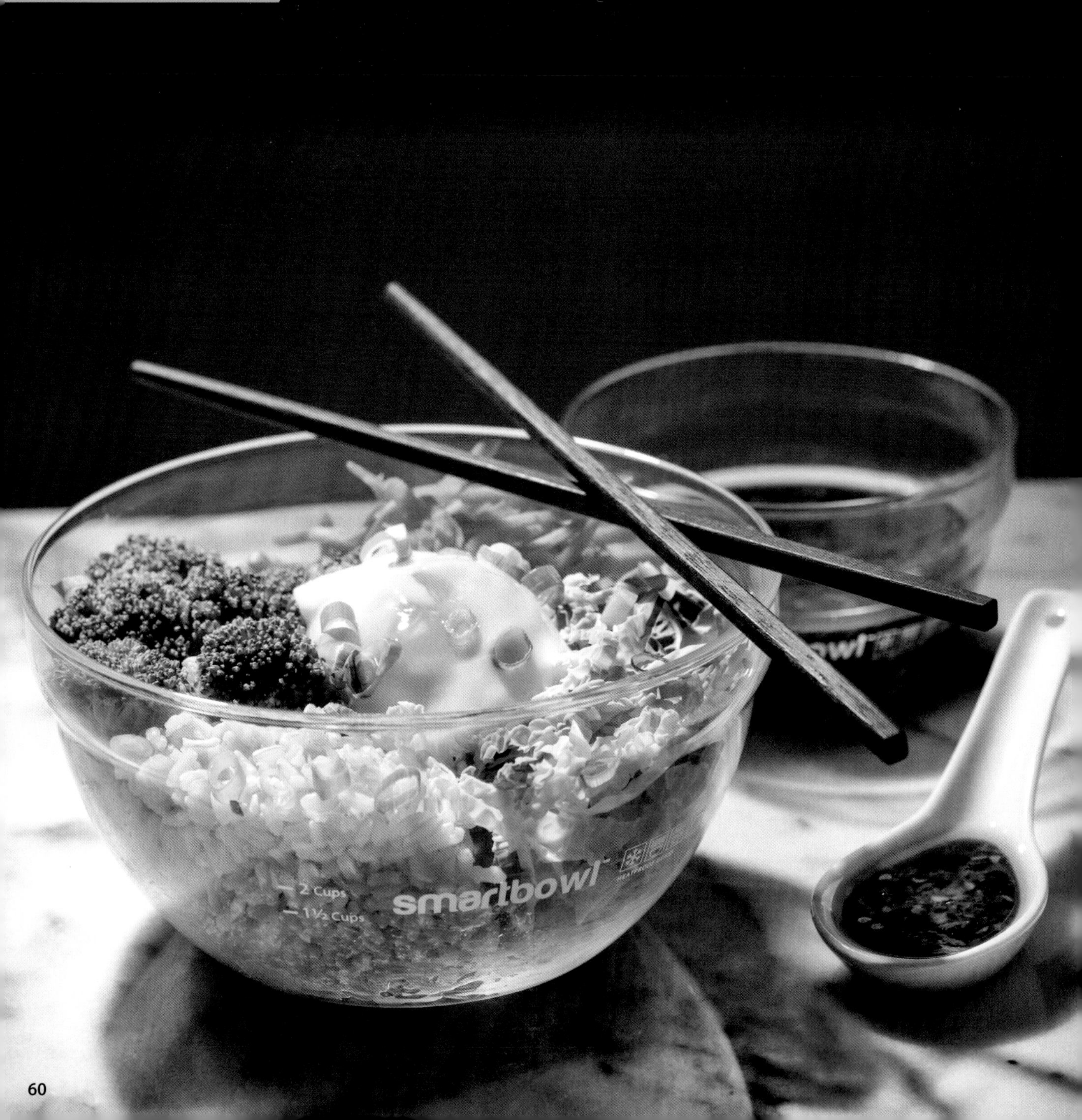
2 Cups
1½ Cups
smartbowl

SERVINGS | 4 LARGE
PREP TIME | 10 MINUTES
COOK TIME | ABOUT 7 MINUTES
USE | LARGE SMARTBOWL™

ASIAN RICE BOWLS

ingredients

2 cups broccoli florets

water

4 cups cooked brown rice

$^1/_2$ head Napa cabbage, sliced thin (about 2 cups)

2 carrots, grated or sliced

$^1/_2$ cup Asian Marinade (see page 105)

4 extra large eggs, poached (see page 10)

$^1/_2$ cup scallions, chopped

sesame seeds

directions

1 Place broccoli into the large smartbowl™ and fill water up to the 1 $^1/_2$ cup mark. Place the lid on the smartbowl™, seal it and press the valve to release air. Microwave for 3 minutes. Carefully strain water out of the bowl using a strainer or the lid. CAUTION: Water will be very hot!

2 Divide the brown rice between 4 serving bowls. Top each bowl with broccoli, cabbage, and carrots. Drizzle each bowl with the Asian Marinade.

3 Top bowls with the poached eggs, scallions, and sesame seeds.

SERVINGS | 1
PREP TIME | 5 MINUTES
COOK TIME | ABOUT 1 $\frac{1}{2}$ MINUTES
USE | LARGE SMARTBOWL™

HALIBUT WITH SPINACH & TOMATOES

ingredients

2 cups baby spinach leaves, loosely packed

1 clove garlic, chopped

³/₄ cup grape tomatoes, cut in half

1 tablespoon water

6 ounces halibut, or other white fish

kosher salt and black pepper

2 teaspoons olive oil

¹/₂ lemon

1 tablespoon fresh basil, chopped

directions

1 Place the spinach, garlic and tomatoes in the large smartbowl™ with 1 tablespoon of water. Season the halibut with salt and pepper and place on top of the vegetables. Drizzle the olive oil over the halibut. Place the lid on, push down to seal and press the valve to release air. Microwave for about 1 ¹/₂ minutes. If not done, add time in 15-second intervals until finished cooking.

2 Carefully remove the smartbowl™ from the microwave. Squeeze the lemon over the halibut and vegetables and top with the fresh basil.

SERVINGS | 1
PREP TIME | 5 MINUTES
COOK TIME | ABOUT 2 MINUTES
USE | LARGE SMARTBOWL™

SALMON & KALE

ingredients

8 leaves kale, torn into small pieces

kosher salt and black pepper

6- to 8-ounce wild salmon, skin on

1 lemon, cut in half, zested

salt and pepper

extra virgin olive oil

directions

1   Place kale into the large smartbowl™. Place salmon on top of kale. Squeeze juice from lemon on top of the salmon and kale. Season with salt and pepper. Place the lid on, push down to seal and press the valve to release air. Microwave for 2 minutes. Test for doneness (more time may be needed for well-done salmon).

2   Drizzle with olive oil, sprinkle with lemon zest and serve.

TIP: If using salmon without skin, reduce the cooking time. Microwave for $1^{1}/_{2}$ minutes. Test doneness. Add time in 15 second intervals, if needed.

SERVINGS | 2
PREP TIME | 5 MINUTES
COOK TIME | ABOUT 3 MINUTES
USE | MEDIUM AND LARGE SMARTBOWL™

SALSA VERDE SHRIMP TACOS

ingredients

12 large shrimp, peeled and deveined

$1/3$ cup store-bought salsa verde

8 small corn tortillas, warm

$1/2$ small avocado, sliced

2 tablespoon chopped white onion

2 tablespoons cilantro leaves

1 lime, cut in half

directions

1 Place the shrimp and salsa verde in the medium smartbowl™. Place the lid on, push down to seal and press the valve to release air. Microwave for $2\,1/2$ minutes or until the shrimp are just cooked.

2 Warm tortillas: Place tortillas in large smartbowl™. Microwave uncovered for 15 seconds.

3 Assemble 4 tacos by doubling two corn tortillas for each taco. Place the shrimp, avocado, white onion, and cilantro on top of each taco. Squeeze the lime and spoon some of the salsa verde on each of the 4 tacos. Serve.

SERVINGS | 4
PREP TIME | 5 MINUTES
COOK TIME | ABOUT 5 MINUTES
USE | MEDIUM AND LARGE SMARTBOWL™

LOW-COUNTRY SHRIMP & GRITS

ingredients

1 cup instant grits

1 cup water

1 cup milk

1 cup grated white cheddar cheese

kosher salt and black pepper

16 medium shrimp, peeled and deveined

$^1/_4$ teaspoon smoky paprika

$^1/_8$ teaspoon cayenne pepper

1 large garlic clove, sliced

2 tablespoons extra virgin olive oil

kosher salt and black pepper

2 teaspoons jalapeño pepper, seeded, ribs removed, diced

2 tablespoons chives, chopped

directions

1 To make grits: Place grits, water, and milk in the large smartbowl™ and stir together to remove any lumps. Place the lid on the smartbowl™, seal the lid, and press the valve to release air. Cook for 2 minutes, stir and cook for 2 more minutes.

2 Remove from the microwave and let sit for 5 minutes with the lid on. Remove the lid. Fold in the cheese and add salt and pepper to taste.

3 To cook the shrimp: Place shrimp, paprika, cayenne pepper, garlic, olive oil, and jalapeño in the medium smartbowl™. Season with salt and pepper. Place the lid on the smartbowl™, seal the lid, and press the valve to release air. Shake to coat the shrimp with the spices. Microwave for 1–1 $^1/_2$ minutes. Check for doneness. Add time in 20 second intervals, until cooked.

4 Serve shrimp on top of warm grits. Extra grits may be stored in the smartbowl™ in the refrigerator to be reheated later.

SERVINGS | 2
PREP TIME | 15 MINUTES
COOK TIME | ABOUT 4 MINUTES
USE | LARGE SMARTBOWL™

NEW ENGLAND LOBSTER BOIL

ingredients

3/4 cup peeled Yukon Gold potatoes, diced

8 green beans

2 teaspoons extra virgin olive oil

kosher salt and pepper

1 cob of corn, cut into 2-inch pieces

pinch of Old Bay® Seasoning

1 clove garlic, sliced

1 bay leaf

2, 4- to 5-ounce ounce lobster tails, shell on, cut in half down the length of the tail

1/2 lemon

directions

1　Place the potatoes, green beans and olive oil in the large smartbowl™ and season with salt and pepper. Place the lid on, push down to seal and press the valve to release air. Microwave for 2 minutes.

2　Add the corn, Old Bay®, garlic, bay leaf and lobster to the bowl with the potatoes and green beans. Place the lid on, push down to seal and press the valve to release air. Microwave for 2 minutes. Carefully remove the smartbowl™ from the microwave and squeeze the lemon juice over the lobster. Serve immediately.

SERVINGS | 2
PREP TIME | 10 MINUTES
COOK TIME | ABOUT 5 MINUTES
USE | MEDIUM AND LARGE SMARTBOWL™

LINGUINE & MUSSELS

ingredients

4 $^1/_2$ ounces linguine pasta, fresh

1 cup water

2 tablespoons extra virgin olive oil, divided

1 large garlic clove, chopped

$^1/_2$ small shallot, sliced thinly

$^1/_2$ cup white wine

about 12 mussels, scrubbed

$^1/_8$ teaspoon red pepper flakes, or to taste

$^1/_4$ cup flat-leaf parsley, chopped

kosher salt and black pepper

$^1/_2$ lemon, juiced

directions

1 Place the linguine in the large smartbowl™ and add 1 cup water, cover and microwave for 2 $^1/_2$ minutes or until the linguine is al dente.

2 Carefully take the smartbowl™ out of the microwave. Toss linguine with salt and pepper and 1 tablespoon olive oil and transfer to the medium smartbowl™. There is no need to strain the linguine. Place the lid over the smartbowl™ to keep warm. Set aside.

3 Using the same smartbowl™ in which you cooked the linguine (no need to wash!), add 1 tablespoon olive oil, shallots, wine, mussels and red pepper flakes. Place the lid on the smartbowl™, seal it and press the valve to release air. Microwave for 2 minutes. Remove smartbowl™ from the microwave, making sure the mussels are open.

4 To serve: Toss mussels with linguine and parsley, adjust for salt and pepper, then squeeze lemon over the pasta.

SERVINGS | 1–2
PREP TIME | 5 MINUTES
COOK TIME | ABOUT 6 MINUTES
USE | LARGE SMARTBOWL™

SAUSAGE & PEPPERS

ingredients

2, 4 ounce chicken sausages

$1/2$ green pepper, sliced

$1/2$ red pepper, sliced

2 teaspoons extra virgin olive oil

$1/2$ cup sliced onions

1 clove garlic, sliced

$1/3$ cup tomato or pasta sauce

2 sprigs fresh oregano

kosher salt and black pepper

crusty bread

directions

1 Puncture sausages with a knife or fork. Set aside.

2 In the large smartbowl™, toss peppers with olive oil, onions and garlic. Place the lid on the smartbowl™, seal the lid, and press valve to release air. Microwave for 1$1/2$ minutes.

3 Remove the smartbowl™ from the microwave and pour tomato sauce on top of the peppers and onions, and then place sausages on top of the sauce. Place the lid on the smartbowl™, seal the lid, and press valve to release air. Microwave until sausages are cooked through and juices run clear, about 4$1/2$ minutes.

4 To serve: place the sausage on a plate and cover with red sauce and vegetables. Adjust for seasoning and garnish with fresh oregano. Serve crusty bread on the side.

SERVINGS | 2
PREP TIME | 15 MINUTES
COOK TIME | ABOUT 7 MINUTES
USE | MEDIUM AND LARGE SMARTBOWL™

MEATBALLS WITH CREAMY POLENTA & RED SAUCE

ingredients

¹⁄₄ **pound ground pork**

¹⁄₄ **pound ground beef**

¹⁄₄ **cup chopped white onion**

1 clove garlic, chopped

2 tablespoons panko bread crumbs

1 tablespoon chopped fresh oregano

1 egg yolk

kosher salt and black pepper

2 teaspoons olive oil

¹⁄₂ **cup store-bought tomato sauce or pasta sauce**

Creamy Polenta (see page 55)

2 tablespoons fresh basil, chopped

directions

1   Combine the ground pork, beef, onion, garlic, bread crumbs, oregano, and egg yolk in a mixing bowl and season with salt and pepper. Form into 8 golf ball size meatballs.

2   Cook the meatballs in 2 batches: Place 1 teaspoon olive oil in the bottom of the large smartbowl™. Place 4 of the meatballs in the smartbowl™ and place the lid on, push down to seal and press the valve to release air. Microwave for 2 minutes and check for doneness. Add time in 15 second intervals until the meatballs are just cooked. Take the meatballs out of the large smartbowl™ and place in the medium smartbowl™ with the lid on to keep warm.

3   Repeat Step 2 for second batch of 4 meatballs.

4   Combine all 8 meatballs and tomato sauce into the large smartbowl™. Stir and microwave for 45 seconds.

5   To serve: Spoon some of the hot polenta on each plate, top with the meatballs, and spoon the cooking juices and tomato sauce over the meatballs. Sprinkle the chopped basil over the meatballs.

SERVINGS | 1–2
PREP TIME | 15 MINUTES
COOK TIME | ABOUT 25 MINUTES
USE | LARGE SMARTBOWL™

CHICKEN CACCIATORE

ingredients

2 boneless, skinless chicken thighs

kosher salt and black pepper

2 teaspoons extra virgin olive oil

$1/2$ cup canned chopped tomatoes

$1/2$ cup pasta sauce

$1/3$ cup chopped white onion

$1/3$ cup chopped red bell pepper

1 tablespoon oregano, chopped

2 tablespoons white wine

1 tablespoons capers, chopped

1 clove garlic, chopped

4 cremini mushrooms, sliced

directions

This recipe is partially made in the oven. Whether food is cooked in the oven or the microwave, the smartbowl™ system infuses moisture for juicy results.

1   Preheat oven to 425°F.

2   Season the chicken thighs with salt and pepper and place one thigh around the side and the other on the bottom of the large smartbowl™. Drizzle with 2 teaspoons of olive oil. Place the lid on the smartbowl™, seal it and press the valve to release air. Place the smartbowl™ on a cookie sheet and in the oven. Bake for 12 minutes. Flip the chicken and bake for about 10 more minutes, or until the chicken is just cooked. Transfer the chicken to a dish.

3   Place the remaining ingredients in the large smartbowl™ with the juices from the chicken. Place the lid on, push down to seal and press the valve to release air. Microwave for 3 minutes. Season to taste with salt and pepper.

4   Cover the chicken with the cacciatore sauce and serve.

SERVINGS | 1–2
PREP TIME | 5 MINUTES
COOK TIME | ABOUT 1 $\frac{1}{2}$ MINUTES PLUS OVERNIGHT
USE | MEDIUM AND LARGE SMARTBOWL™

WEEKNIGHT CHICKEN BREAST

ingredients

8 ounces boneless, skinless chicken breast, cut into strips

kosher salt and black pepper

$\frac{1}{4}$ cup 5-Minute Marinade of your choice (see page 105)

directions

1 Season chicken lightly with salt and pepper. Place the chicken in the medium smartbowl™ and add $\frac{1}{4}$ cup of marinade. Push lid down and pinch the valve to release air. Shake. Store refrigerated, overnight.

2 Remove half the strips of chicken from the marinade and arrange them along the sides of the large smartbowl™, placing any left over pieces on the bottom, being careful not to overlap strips. Push lid down and pinch the valve to release air.

3 Microwave for 30 to 45 seconds. Check doneness, cook for up to 1 additional minute, in 15 second intervals until done.

4 Repeat steps 1-3 for the second half of the chicken breast.

ENTERTAINING

SERVINGS | 6
PREP TIME | 5 MINUTES
COOK TIME | ABOUT 2 $1/2$ MINUTES
USE | LARGE SMARTBOWL™

SPINACH DIP

ingredients

6 ounces frozen spinach, thawed

6 ounces canned artichokes, drained and chopped

$1/2$ cup cream cheese

2 tablespoons mayonnaise

$1/3$ cup sour cream

$1/2$ cup grated Parmesan cheese, divided

Dash of hot sauce (optional)

1 teaspoon lemon zest

kosher salt and black pepper

Serve with vegetables— peppers, carrots, grape tomatoes, celery, zucchini, asparagus, jicama etc.

directions

1   Preheat oven to broil.

2   Place the frozen spinach and artichokes in the large smartbowl™. Place the lid on, push down to seal and press the valve to release air. Microwave for 2 minutes. Remove from microwave and drain any liquid carefully—it will be hot.

3   Add the cream cheese, place the lid on, push down to seal and press the valve to release air. Microwave for 30 seconds.

4   Carefully remove from the microwave and stir. Add the mayonnaise, sour cream, parmesan cheese, hot sauce and lemon zest. Season to taste with salt and pepper.

5   Sprinkle with remaining Parmesan cheese. Place on a cookie sheet and set under the broiler, uncovered, for 3 to 4 minutes until golden brown. Serve with vegetables.

SERVINGS | 2
PREP TIME | 5 MINUTES
COOK TIME | ABOUT 2 $^1/_2$ MINUTES
USE | LARGE SMARTBOWL™

WHOLE "ROASTED" GARLIC

ingredients

1 garlic bulb, top cut off

$^1/_4$ cup milk

$^1/_4$ cup extra virgin olive oil

2 sprigs thyme

kosher salt

your favorite crusty bread

directions

1 Place the garlic cut side down in the large smartbowl™ and add the milk. Place the lid on, push down to seal and press the valve to release air. Microwave for about 1 $^1/_2$ minutes.

2 Remove from the microwave and drain the milk carefully. Add the olive oil and thyme. Place the lid on, push down to seal and press the valve to release air. Microwave for 2 minutes cut side down, or until soft when punctured with a knife. Add time in 30-second intervals.

3 Remove smartbowl™ from the microwave. Let cool and squeeze out the garlic clove, smash with a knife, season with salt and add the olive oil from cooking. Serve with a great baguette or ciabatta.

TIP: Cooking time depends on the size and age of the head of garlic you are using.

SERVINGS | 4
PREP TIME | 10 MINUTES
COOK TIME | ABOUT 3 MINUTES
USE | MEDIUM SMARTBOWL™

LIMA BEAN & LEEK SPREAD WITH PARMESAN CHEESE

ingredients

9 ounces frozen lima beans, thawed

$1/2$ cup leeks, cleaned and chopped, white part only

pinch of salt

4 tablespoons extra virgin olive oil, divided

$1/2$ garlic clove

2 ounces Parmesan cheese, grated, with extra for serving

2 tablespoons mint leaves

2 tablespoons lemon juice, freshly squeezed

kosher salt and black pepper

directions

1   Place lima beans, leeks, and 1 tablespoon of olive oil in the medium smartbowl™. Season with salt. Place the lid on the smartbowl™, seal the lid, and press valve to release air. Microwave for 1 minute.

2   Remove smartbowl™ from the microwave, and add 2 tablespoons of water to the contents of the smartbowl™. Place the lid on the smartbowl™, seal the lid, and press valve to release air. Microwave for 2 minutes.

3   Blend the lima beans, 2 tablespoons of olive oil, garlic, Parmesan cheese, mint, and lemon juice to preferred smoothness. Season with salt and pepper.

4   Drizzle with remaining 1 tablespoon of olive oil and Parmesan cheese. Serve with freshly cut vegetables or crostini.

QUANTITY | 2–3 CUPS
PREP TIME | 2 MINUTES
COOK TIME | 6 MINUTES
USE | LARGE SMARTBOWL™

ROSEMARY THYME CARAMEL POPCORN

ingredients

1 ½ tablespoons popcorn kernels

2 tablespoons butter, unsalted

1 sprig of rosemary

2 sprigs of thyme

2 tablespoons maple syrup

¼ cup brown sugar

¼ teaspoon salt, or to taste

¼ teaspoon baking soda

1 ½ tablespoons heavy cream

directions

1 Line a baking sheet with buttered parchment paper or a silicone mat. Set aside.

2 Place 1 ½ tablespoons of popcorn kernels in the large smartbowl™. Place the lid on the smartbowl™, seal it and press the valve to release air. Microwave for 2 minutes or until all the kernels are popped. Pour the popcorn into another container and set aside.

3 Place butter, rosemary and thyme in the large smartbowl™. Place the lid on the smartbowl™, seal the lid, and press valve to release air. Microwave for about 25 seconds. Remove from the microwave, remove rosemary and thyme with a fork, and stir to melt.

4 Add maple syrup, brown sugar, and salt. Stir to incorporate. Place the lid on the smartbowl™, seal the lid, and press valve to release air. Microwave for 1 ½ minutes or until sugar dissolves.

5 Carefully take the smartbowl™ out of the microwave. Place a folded kitchen towel over the smartbowl™ and remove the lid.

6 Immediately sprinkle baking soda into the smartbowl™ and whisk quickly, being careful as caramelized sugar will bubble up.

7 Whisk in the heavy cream in a slow, steady stream.

8 Pour caramel onto the buttered parchment or silicone mat. Be careful! This is hot!

9 Immediately pour popcorn onto the caramel and fold gently with a spatula and serve.

SERVINGS | 6
PREP TIME | 2 MINUTES
COOK TIME | ABOUT 1 MINUTE
USE | LARGE SMARTBOWL™

WARM BRIE WITH FIG PRESERVES & ALMONDS

ingredients

6 $^1/_2$ ounce wheel baby goat or regular brie (about 4 $^1/_2$ inches round)

$^1/_2$ cup fig jam or preserves

$^1/_4$ cup almonds, skin on, chopped into big chunks

3 sprigs thyme

Garnish: serve with crackers

directions

1 Place the brie in the large smartbowl™ and cover top of cheese wheel with the fig jam and thyme. Place the lid on, push down to seal and press the valve to release air. Microwave for 1 minute.

2 Garnish with the almonds and serve warm, with crackers.

3 To reheat brie, place the lid back on, push down to seal and press the valve to release air. Microwave for 30 seconds.

TIP: Serve with crackers.

DESSERTS

CHEWY ALMOND BUTTER OATMEAL BARS, PAGE 95

SERVINGS | 2–4
PREP TIME | 5 MINUTES
COOK TIME | ABOUT 4 MINUTES
USE | LARGE SMARTBOWL™

OOEY GOOEY MOCHA CHOCOLATE CAKE

ingredients

½ cup chocolate chips

4 tablespoons butter, room temperature

4 tablespoons sugar

1 teaspoon vanilla extract

1 teaspoon coffee, instant

2 tablespoons all-purpose flour

2 extra large eggs, room temperature

ice cream or plain Greek yogurt (optional)

directions

1 Place chocolate chips and butter in the large smartbowl™. Place the lid on the smartbowl™, seal the lid, and press valve to release air. Microwave for 25 seconds.

2 Remove the smartbowl™ from microwave and stir until chocolate and butter are incorporated. If more time is needed to melt the ingredients, add additional cooking time in 15-second increments.

3 Once the chocolate and butter are blended, add sugar, vanilla, coffee, flour, and eggs. Stir until smooth.

4 Place the lid on the smartbowl™ seal the lid, and press valve to release air. Microwave for 2-3 minutes, adding time in 30 second increments, if needed to attain desired doneness.

5 Remove smartbowl™ from the microwave and let sit for about 2 minutes, with the lid on. Cake will be gooey and delicious on the bottom of the smartbowl™. Serve warm, with or without ice cream or plain Greek yogurt.

SERVINGS | 2

PREP TIME | 5 MINUTES

COOK TIME | ABOUT 1 MINUTE, PLUS 1 $^1/_2$ HOURS REFRIGERATED STORAGE

USE | SMALL AND MEDIUM SMARTBOWL™

CHOCOLATE PUDDING WITH POMEGRANATE & CHIA SEED TOPPING

ingredients

Pudding:

$^1/_2$ **cup semi-sweet chocolate chips**

$^1/_4$ **cup coconut milk**

1 tablespoon honey

fresh berries

To make Pomegranate Chia Seed Topping:

1 tablespoon chia seeds

$^1/_4$ **cup pomegranate juice**

directions

1 To make pudding: place chocolate, coconut milk and honey in the medium smartbowl™. Mix well and place the lid on, push down to seal and press the valve to release air. Microwave for 1 minute and stir. If not melted through, microwave in 15-second intervals, being very careful not to overheat chocolate. Once melted, mix well.

2 Chill in refrigerator until set, at least 1 $^1/_2$ hours.

3 To make Pomegranate Chia Seed Topping: combine chia seeds and pomegranate juice in a small smartbowl™ and allow to sit and bloom for at least 15 minutes, or until the chia seeds absorb the moisture and become thick and gelatinous, like a pudding.

4 To serve: spoon chocolate pudding into serving bowls and top with Pomegranate Chia Seed Topping and fresh berries.

TIP: For individual serving portions, pour pudding into serving dishes before refrigerating.

SERVINGS | 2
PREP TIME | 5 MINUTES
COOK TIME | ABOUT 4 $^1/_2$ MINUTES
USE | SMALL, MEDIUM AND LARGE SMARTBOWL™

FALL-SPICED APPLES

ingredients

2 teaspoons unsalted butter

$^1/_2$ teaspoon cinnamon or pumpkin spice

pinch of nutmeg

2 teaspoons maple syrup

1 tablespoon dried fruit, chopped into a paste

1 tablespoon almonds, toasted and finely chopped

2 small apples

$^1/_4$ cup water

1 tablespoon lemon juice

directions

1 Place butter, cinnamon, nutmeg, and maple syrup into the small smartbowl™. Place the lid on the smartbowl™, seal the lid, and press valve to release air. Microwave for 30 seconds.

2 Remove the smartbowl™ from the microwave and add the dried fruit paste and almonds. Stir and set aside.

3 Cut off the bottom part of the apples, about $^1/_4$ inch, so that the apples stand easily on their own. Peel each apple and core $^3/_4$ of the way through.

4 In the medium smartbowl™, add water and lemon juice. Dip and roll each apple in the water and lemon mixture to prevent apples from turning brown.

5 Place apples in the large smartbowl™. Stir the dried fruit and spice mixture. Carefully spoon the dried fruit mixture into the cavity of each apple. The apples should be filled with more dried fruit than liquid. Reserve the remaining liquid for serving.

6 Once apples are filled, place the lid on the smartbowl™, seal the lid, and press valve to release air. Microwave for 4 minutes or longer if you prefer softer apples.

7 To serve: place one apple on each plate and spoon the sauce onto the apples for garnish.

SERVINGS | 4
PREP TIME | 10 MINUTES
COOK TIME | ABOUT 20 MINUTES
USE | MEDIUM AND LARGE SMARTBOWL™

PEACH & BLUEBERRY CRISP

ingredients

1 ¹/₂ cups dried oatmeal

¹/₈ teaspoon ground cinnamon

¹/₄ cup light brown sugar

¹/₃ cup cold butter, cubed

pinch of salt

1 ¹/₂ cups sliced frozen peaches

1 ¹/₂ cups frozen blueberries

2 teaspoons cornstarch

Optional: ice cream

directions

1   Preheat the oven to 425°F.

2   To make the crisp topping: in the medium smartbowl™, combine the oatmeal, cinnamon, brown sugar, cold butter and salt. Mix with your fingers until crumbly and fully combined. Set aside.

3   Place the frozen peaches and blueberries in the large smartbowl™ and toss with the cornstarch. Place the lid on, push down to seal and press the valve to release air. Microwave for 5 minutes, stirring once at 3 minutes.

4   Carefully remove the smartbowl™ from the microwave and top with the oatmeal mixture. Place the smartbowl™ on a cookie sheet and bake in the oven, uncovered for 15 minutes or until the topping is crisp and golden brown.

5   Remove from the oven and enjoy warm, or with ice cream.

TIP: the crisp topping can be made in a food processor. Add oatmeal, cinnamon, brown sugar and salt to the processor. Pulse until combined. Add cold butter and pulse until it looks like coarse crumbs.

QUANTITY | $\frac{1}{2}$ CUP
PREP TIME | 2 MINUTES
COOK TIME | ABOUT 2 MINUTES
USE | MEDIUM SMARTBOWL™

MEXICAN SPICED CHOCOLATE SAUCE

ingredients

Mexican Spiced Chocolate Blend:

2 tablespoons cocoa powder

1 teaspoon cinnamon

$\frac{1}{8}$ teaspoon cayenne pepper, or to taste

pinch of salt

Mexican Spiced Chocolate Sauce:

1 $\frac{1}{2}$ tablespoons butter

$\frac{1}{4}$ cup of sugar

1 tablespoon Mexican Chocolate Spice Blend

1 $\frac{1}{2}$ tablespoons heavy cream, or to taste

directions

1   For the spice blend: Place all items in a medium smartbowl™ and cover. Shake well until all ingredients are blended.

2   For the chocolate sauce: Place the butter in a large smartbowl™. Place the lid on the smartbowl™, seal it and press the valve to release air. Microwave for about 25 seconds. Remove from the microwave and stir to melt.

3   Stir the sugar into the melted butter mixture. Place the lid on the smartbowl™, seal it and press the valve to release air. Microwave for about 1 $\frac{1}{2}$ minutes. Carefully remove from the microwave and stir to melt.

4   Add the Mexican Spiced Chocolate Blend until fully incorporated, then slowly whisk in heavy cream.

TIP: Drizzle over popcorn and serve.

SERVINGS | 8
PREP TIME | 5 MINUTES
COOK TIME | ABOUT 1 MINUTE
USE | MEDIUM AND LARGE SMARTBOWL™

CHEWY ALMOND BUTTER & OATMEAL BARS

ingredients

2 cups old-fashioned oats

1 ¹/₂ cups crispy rice cereal

1 ¹/₄ cup chunky almond butter

³/₄ cup honey

¹/₄ cup light brown sugar

¹/₈ teaspoon kosher salt

1 teaspoon vanilla extract

2 tablespoons almonds, chopped

melted dark chocolate for garnish

directions

1 Line an 8 x 8-inch baking dish with aluminum foil. In a mixing bowl, toss together the oats and crispy rice cereal and set aside.

2 Place the almond butter, honey, brown sugar, salt and vanilla in the large smartbowl™. Place the lid on, push down to seal and press the valve to release air. Microwave for 1 ¹/₂ minutes. Remove from the microwave and stir the ingredients until fully combined. Add almonds and stir.

3 Pour the almond butter mixture into the crispy rice cereal and oats mixture and stir together until fully combined. Spoon the mixture into the prepared pan and refrigerate for 30 minutes or until firm. Cut into bars and drizzle with the melted chocolate. Store in the refrigerator.

4 Melted dark chocolate: put ¹/₂ cup of semi-sweet chocolate chips in the medium smartbowl™. Place the lid on, push down to seal and press valve to release air. Microwave for 20 seconds. Remove from the microwave and stir.

SERVINGS | 4
PREP TIME | 5 MINUTES
COOK TIME | ABOUT 2 $^3/_4$ MINUTES
USE | LARGE SMARTBOWL™

PEANUT BUTTER CUP COOKIES

ingredients

2 teaspoons butter, softened

2 tablespoons smooth peanut butter

4 tablespoons light brown sugar

pinch of kosher salt

$^1/_2$ teaspoon vanilla extract

2 extra large egg yolks, room temperature

2 teaspoons coconut milk or whole milk, room temperature

6 tablespoons all-purpose flour

2 tablespoons old-fashioned oats

4 tablespoons chocolate chips

Optional: ice cream

directions

1   Place butter and peanut butter in the large smartbowl™. Place the lid on the smartbowl™, seal the lid, and press the valve to release air. Microwave for about 20 seconds or until melted. Carefully remove the smartbowl™ from the microwave.

2   Add sugar, salt, vanilla, egg yolks, milk, flour, and oats to the smartbowl™ and stir until thoroughly mixed. Fold chocolate chips into the batter and flatten the top down. Place the lid on the smartbowl™, seal the lid, and press the valve to release air. Microwave for about 1 minute, 30 seconds.

3   Carefully remove the smartbowl™ from the microwave. Set aside, with the lid on, for 2 minutes to allow the cookies to finish cooking in the smartbowl™.

4   Serve warm, or with ice cream.

PANTRY

SMITH FAMILY GARDEN PICKLES, PAGE 98

QUANTITY | 1 CUP

PREP TIME | 3 MINUTES PLUS 5 HOUR/OVERNIGHT REFRIGERATED STORAGE

USE | LARGE SMARTBOWL™

SMITH FAMILY GARDEN PICKLES

ingredients

1 cup assorted vegetables such as cucumbers, green tomatoes, peppers, and cauliflower, cut into slices

Pickling Liquid:

$1/2$ cup white wine vinegar

$1/2$ cup apple cider vinegar

pickling spices (entire amount made from the recipe below)

Pickling Spices:

1 teaspoon pickling or non-iodized salt

$1/4$ teaspoon coriander

$1/4$ teaspoon mustard seeds

1 allspice berry

$1/4$ cinnamon stick

1 bay leaf

directions

1 Mix all of the ingredients for the pickling liquid in a bowl.

2 Arrange vegetables on the bottom of a large smartbowl™.

3 Pour pickling liquid to cover. Place the lid on the smartbowl™, seal the lid, and press valve to release air.

4 Refrigerate overnight or at least 5 hours before serving.

QUANTITY | 1 CUP
PREP TIME | 5 MINUTES
COOK TIME | ABOUT 3 ½ MINUTES PLUS 3 HOURS/OVERNIGHT REFRIGERATED STORAGE
USE | LARGE SMARTBOWL™

COOKED PICKLED BEETS

ingredients

1 cup red beets, peeled and sliced about ½ inch thick

½ cup water

Pickling Liquid:

½ cup white wine vinegar

½ cup apple cider vinegar

pickling spices (entire amount made from the recipe below)

Pickling Spices:

1 teaspoon pickling or non-iodized salt

¼ teaspoon fennel

¼ teaspoon mustard seeds

1 allspice berry

¼ cinnamon stick

1 bay leaf

directions

1 Mix all of the ingredients for the pickling liquid in a bowl.

2 Place beets and water into the large smartbowl™. Place the lid on the smartbowl™, seal it, and press the valve to release the air. Microwave for about 4 minutes, or until beets are tender. Leave covered for about 5 minutes.

3 Remove the lid, drain the water and cool the beets. Add the pickling liquid and refrigerate overnight or at least 5 hours before serving. Reserve the liquid for more pickles.

QUANTITY | ¹/₂ CUP
PREP TIME | 5 MINUTES
COOK TIME | ABOUT 5 MINUTES
USE | SMALL, MEDIUM SMARTBOWL™

CARAMELIZED ONIONS

ingredients

¹/₄ large onion, sliced (about ¹/₂ cup)

1 tablespoon butter

pinch of salt

directions

1 In the medium smartbowl™, mix together sliced onions, 1 tablespoon of butter, and a pinch of salt. Place the lid on the smartbowl™, seal the lid, and press the valve to release air. Microwave for 3 minutes.

2 Take smartbowl™ from microwave, remove lid, and stir contents. Replace the lid, sealing as before, and repeat this process at 1-minute intervals for another 2 minutes until caramelized. If onions need more time, add time in 30-second intervals until onions are caramelized.

QUANTITY | 1 CUP
PREP TIME | 5 MINUTES
USE | SMALL SMARTBOWL™

GREEN GODDESS DRESSING

ingredients

¾ cup Greek yogurt

2 anchovy filets, packed in water

1 scallion, chopped

1 ½ tablespoons parsley

1 ½ tablespoons chives

2 tablespoons extra virgin olive oil

1 tablespoon lemon juice

1 teaspoon fresh tarragon or basil, chopped

kosher salt and black pepper

directions

1   Puree all ingredients in a food processor or blender. Season with salt and pepper—but remember, anchovy filets can be salty.

2   Store dressing in the small smartbowl™ in the refrigerator for about a week.

QUANTITY | ABOUT ¹/₂ CUP
PREP TIME | 4 MINUTES
USE | SMALL SMARTBOWL™

MEDITERRANEAN SALAD DRESSING

ingredients

5 tablespoons extra virgin olive oil

3 tablespoons fresh lemon juice

¹/₂ tablespoon garlic clove, crushed

1 tablespoon of Mediterranean Spice Blend (see page 107)

kosher salt and black pepper

directions

1   Place all ingredients in the small smartbowl™. Place the lid on the smartbowl™, seal and shake contents until well blended. Season with salt and pepper.

QUANTITY | ABOUT $\frac{1}{2}$ CUP
PREP TIME | 5 MINUTES
USE | SMALL SMARTBOWL™

ORANGE VINAIGRETTE

ingredients

3 tablespoons of fresh-squeezed orange juice

2 tablespoons extra virgin olive oil

1 tablespoon champagne or white wine vinegar

2 teaspoons fresh tarragon, chopped

2 teaspoons of chives, chopped

pinch kosher salt

directions

1 Place all ingredients in the medium smartbowl™. Place the lid on the smartbowl™, seal and shake contents until well blended. Store in the refrigerator.

5-MINUTE MARINADES

QUANTITY | 1 CUP
PREP TIME | 5 MINUTES
USE | SMALL SMARTBOWL™

Dijon Mustard Marinade

ingredients

2 cloves garlic, minced

2 tablespoons Dijon mustard

1 tablespoon white wine vinegar (or apple cider vinegar)

2 tablespoons extra virgin olive oil

2 teaspoons honey

1 tablespoon Mediterranean Herb Blend (see page 107)

kosher salt and white pepper

directions

Place all ingredients in the medium smartbowl™, mix well, and season with salt and pepper. Refrigerate in smartbowl™ until ready to use.

QUANTITY | 1 CUP
PREP TIME | 5 MINUTES
USE | SMALL SMARTBOWL™

Asian Marinade

ingredients

3 tablespoons Tamari or low-sodium soy sauce

2 tablespoon rice wine vinegar

1 tablespoon sesame oil

1 tablespoon garlic, grated or minced

1 tablespoon ginger, grated or minced

1 teaspoon crushed red pepper flakes

directions

Place all ingredients in the small smartbowl™. Cover and shake well. Refrigerate in smartbowl™ until ready to use.

QUANTITY | 1 CUP
PREP TIME | 5 MINUTES
USE | SMALL SMARTBOWL™

Tandoori Marinade

ingredients

1 cup plain yogurt, full fat

1 inch piece of ginger root, peeled and grated (about 1 $^1/_2$ tablespoons)

$^1/_2$ lemon, juiced

$^1/_2$ lemon zest, grated

$^1/_2$ tablespoon Indian Spice Blend (see page 107)

$^1/_4$ teaspoon chili or red pepper flakes, to taste

kosher salt and black pepper

directions

Mix all ingredients in the small smartbowl™ and season with salt and pepper. Stir. Refrigerate in smartbowl™ until ready to use.

I hope you enjoy these flavorful marinades that you can keep refrigerated in your smartbowl™ for up to a week and use as a marinade and as part of dressings and sauces in other recipes in this book.

2-MINUTE SPICE BLENDS

QUANTITY | 3 TABLESPOONS
PREP TIME | 2 MINUTES
USE | SMALL SMARTBOWL™

Indian Spice Blend

ingredients

1 tablespoon ground cumin

1 tablespoon ground coriander

1 teaspoon ground cardamom

1 teaspoon ground black pepper

1 teaspoon cinnamon

$^{1}/_{4}$ teaspoon cloves

$^{1}/_{4}$ teaspoon ground nutmeg

$^{1}/_{4}$ teaspoon turmeric

kosher salt and black pepper

directions

Place all ingredients in the small smartbowl™. Cover, shake well, and store.

QUANTITY | 3 TABLESPOONS
PREP TIME | 2 MINUTES
USE | SMALL SMARTBOWL™

Mediterranean Herb Blend

ingredients

2 tablespoons dried thyme

1 tablespoon dried oregano

$^{1}/_{2}$ tablespoon dried rosemary

1 teaspoon dried marjoram

directions

Place all ingredients in the small smartbowl™. Cover, shake well, and store.

QUANTITY | 3 TABLESPOONS
PREP TIME | 2 MINUTES
USE | SMALL SMARTBOWL™

Moroccan Spice Blend

ingredients

2 teaspoons cumin

2 teaspoons ground ginger

1 teaspoon ground cinnamon

1 teaspoon ground coriander

$^{1}/_{2}$ teaspoon ground black pepper

$^{1}/_{4}$ teaspoon ground cloves

directions

Place all ingredients in the small smartbowl™. Cover, shake well, and store.

Cooking smart has to be something that's time-efficient and brings a whole lot of flavor without a whole lot of effort. I believe in banning boredom in the kitchen. These herb and spice blends can serve as rubs but also as the secret ingredients for some of the recipes and marinades in the book.

Use fresh spices, mix them, throw them, push the valve of your tiny smartbowl™ and shake. This keeps for a while but I have the feeling you'll have to make more soon.

5-MINUTE BABY FOOD
(For babies 10 months and older)

Pea Puree

PREP TIME | 2 MINUTES
COOK TIME | ABOUT 2 MINUTES
USE | MEDIUM SMARTBOWL™

ingredients

½ cup frozen peas, thawed

2 tablespoons water

directions

1 Place peas and water into the medium smartbowl™. Place the lid on the smartbowl™, seal it and press the valve to release air. Microwave for 2 minutes.

2 Check for doneness. If not cooked, add time in 20 second intervals.

3 When done, use an immersion blender to puree into desired consistency.

Sweet Potato Puree

PREP TIME | 2 MINUTES
COOK TIME | ABOUT 3 MINUTES
USE | MEDIUM SMARTBOWL™

ingredients

¹/₂ cup sweet potatoes, chopped

2 tablespoons water

directions

1 Place sweet potato and water into the medium smartbowl™. Place the lid on the smartbowl™, seal it and press the valve to release air. Microwave for 3 minutes.

2 Check for doneness. If not cooked, add time in 20 second intervals.

3 When done, use an immersion blender to puree into desired consistency.

Beet Puree

PREP TIME | 2 MINUTES
COOK TIME | ABOUT 1 MINUTE
USE | MEDIUM SMARTBOWL™

ingredients

¹/₂ cup beets, chopped

3 tablespoons water

directions

1 Put beets and water into the medium smartbowl™. Place the lid on the smartbowl™, seal it, and press the valve to release air. Microwave for 4 minutes, and then let sit covered, for about 5 minutes or until the beets are soft.

2 Check for doneness. If not cooked, add time in 20 second intervals.

3 When done, use an immersion blender to puree into desired consistency.

The smartbowl™ system is ideal for keeping baby food fresh and free of hot spots when warmed. Always serve and store in different smartbowls™. Make sure to test the food temperature before feeding baby. Strain purees for younger babies.

Index

A

Almonds:
Chewy Almond Butter & Oatmeal Bars 95
Fall-Spiced Apples 91
Green Beans Almondine 50
Moroccan Couscous 46
Turkey Sausage Stuffed Pears 20
Warm Brie with Fig Preserves & Almonds 84

Appetizers:
Lima Bean Mint Spread Appetizer 82
Rosemary & Thyme Caramel Popcorn 83
Spinach Dip 80
Warm Brie with Fig Preserves & Almonds 84
Whole "Roasted" Garlic 81

Apples:
Creamy Butternut Squash & Apple Soup 39
Fall-Spiced Apples 91

Apricots:
Moroccan Couscous 46

Artichokes:
Spinach Dip 80
Asian Rice Bowls 61

Avocados:
Huevos Rancheros 28
Salsa Verde Shrimp Tacos 66
Turkey Chili 42

B

Baby Food: See 5-Minute Baby Food
Bacon:
Bleu Cheese Omelette with Bacon 26
Braised Kale with Lardons 49
Banana-Pecan Oatmeal, Overnight 23

Beans:
Green Beans Almondine 50
Lima Bean Mint Spread Appetizer 82
New England Lobster Boil 70
Turkey Chili 42

Beef:
Meatballs with Creamy Polenta & Red Sauce 75

Beets:
Beet Puree 109
Cooked Pickled Beets 99
Farmhouse Chopped Salad To-Go 31
Pickled Beet & Orange Salad To-Go 32
Bleu Cheese Omelette with Bacon 26

Blueberries:
Chef Art's Smart Start Blueberry Oatmeal 27
Homemade Blueberry Jam 24

Peach & Blueberry Crisp 92
Braised Kale with Lardons 49
Bread:
Caramelized Onion, Spinach & Gruyere Strata 19
French Toast Bread Pudding 15
Sausage & Peppers 73
Tuscan Tomato Soup 40
Whole "Roasted" Garlic 81

Breakfast:
Bleu Cheese Omelette with Bacon 26
Caramelized Onion, Spinach & Gruyere Strata 19
Chef Art's Smart Start Blueberry Oatmeal 27
Creamy Boursin® Cheese Scrambled Eggs 12
French Toast Bread Pudding 15
Homemade Blueberry Jam 24
Huevos Rancheros 28
Mediterranean Poached Egg 16
Overnight Banana-Pecan Oatmeal 23
Traditional Southern Ham Hash 13
Turkey Sausage Stuffed Pears 20
Brie with Fig Preserves & Almonds, Warm 84

Broccoli:
Asian Rice Bowls 61
Broccoli with Thai Peanut Sauce 51
Brussels Sprouts, Ginger-Soy 48

C

Cabbage:
Asian Rice Bowls 61
Farmhouse Chopped Salad To-Go 31
Cake, Ooey Gooey Mocha Chocolate 87
Caramelized Onions 100
Caramelized Onion, Spinach & Gruyere Strata 19

Carrots:
Asian Rice Bowls 61
Farmhouse Chopped Salad To-Go 31

Cauliflower:
Cauliflower, Leek, & Fennel Soup 37
Chef Art's Garlicky Mashed Cauliflower 53
Chef Art's Garlicky Mashed Cauliflower 53
Chef Art's Smart Start Blueberry Oatmeal 27
Chewy Almond Butter & Oatmeal Bars 95

Chia Seeds:
Chef Art's Smart Start Blueberry Oatmeal 27

Chocolate Pudding with Pomegranate & Chia Seed Topping 88

Chicken:
Chicken Cacciatore 76
Farmhouse Chopped Salad To-Go 31
Sausage & Peppers 73
Weeknight Chicken Breast 78
Chili, Turkey 42

Chocolate:
Chewy Almond Butter & Oatmeal Bars 95
Chocolate Pudding with Pomegranate & Chia Seed Topping 88
Mexican-Spiced Chocolate 94
Ooey Gooey Mocha Chocolate Cake 87
Peanut Butter Cup Cookie 96
Turkey Chili 42
Cooked Pickled Beets 99

Cookies:
Chewy Almond Butter & Oatmeal Bars 95
Peanut Butter Cup Cookie 96

Cooking Charts:
Egg Cooking Charts 10
Veggies Cooking Chart 9

Corn:
New England Lobster Boil 70
Couscous, Moroccan 46
Creamy Boursin® Cheese Scrambled Eggs 12
Creamy Butternut Squash & Apple Soup 39
Creamy Polenta 55

D

Desserts:
Chewy Almond Butter & Oatmeal Bars 95
Chocolate Pudding with Pomegranate & Chia Seed Topping 88
Fall-Spiced Apples 91
Mexican-Spiced Chocolate 94
Ooey Gooey Mocha Chocolate Cake 87
Peach & Blueberry Crisp 92
Peanut Butter Cup Cookie 96
Dijon Mustard Chicken Marinade 105

E

Egg Cooking Charts 10
Eggs:
Asian Rice Bowls 61
Bleu Cheese Omelette with Bacon 26
Caramelized Onion, Spinach & Gruyere Strata 19
Creamy Boursin® Cheese Scrambled Eggs 12

Huevos Rancheros 28
Mediterranean Poached Egg 16
Ooey Gooey Mocha Chocolate Cake 87
Traditional Southern Ham Hash 13
Turkey Sausage Stuffed Pears 20

Entertaining:
  Lima Bean Mint Spread Appetizer 82
  Rosemary & Thyme Caramel Popcorn 83
  Spinach Dip 80
  Warm Brie with Fig Preserves & Almonds 84
  Whole "Roasted" Garlic 81

F
Fall-Spiced Apples 91
Farmhouse Chopped Salad To-Go 31
Fennel Soup, Cauliflower, Leek, & 37
Fingerling Potatoes 58
5-Minute Baby Food:
  Beet Puree 109
  Pea Puree 109
  Sweet Potato Puree 109
5-Minute Marinades:
  Asian Marinade 105
  Dijon Mustard Chicken Marinade 105
  Tandoori Chicken Marinade 105
French Toast Bread Pudding 15

G
Garlic, Whole "Roasted" 81
Ginger-Soy Brussels Sprouts 48
Green Beans Almondine 50
Green Goddess Dressing 101
Grits, Low-Country Shrimp & 69

H
Halibut with Spinach & Tomatoes 62
Ham Hash, Traditional Southern 13
Homemade Blueberry Jam 24
How to cook smart 8
Huevos Rancheros 28

I
Indian Spice Blend 107

J
Jam:
  Homemade Blueberry Jam 24
Jam, Homemade Blueberry 24

K
Kale:
  Braised Kale with Lardons 49
  Salmon & Kale 65

L
Lardons, Braised Kale with 49
Leeks:
  Cauliflower, Leek, & Fennel Soup 37
  Lima Bean Mint Spread Appetizer 82
Lima Bean Mint Spread Appetizer 82
Linguine & Mussels 72
Lobster Boil, New England 70
Low-Country Shrimp & Grits 69

M
Main Courses:
  Asian Rice Bowls 61
  Chicken Cacciatore 76
  Halibut with Spinach & Tomatoes 62
  Linguine & Mussels 72
  Low-Country Shrimp & Grits 69
  Meatballs with Creamy Polenta & Red
    Sauce 75
  New England Lobster Boil 70
  Salmon & Kale 65
  Salsa Verde Shrimp Tacos 66
  Sausage & Peppers 73
  Weeknight Chicken Breast 78
Marinades: See 5-Minute Marinades:
Marshmallows:
  Creamy Butternut Squash & Apple Soup 39
  Sweet Potatoes with Maple Syrup,
    Marshmallows & Rosemary 57
Meatballs with Creamy Polenta & Red
    Sauce 75
Mediterranean Herb Blend 107
Mediterranean Poached Egg 16
Mediterranean Salad Dressing 102
Mediterranean Salad to-Go 35
Mexican-Spiced Chocolate 94
Mint:
  Lima Bean Mint Spread Appetizer 82
  Pea & Summer Squash Soup 41
  Tabbouleh 45
Miso Soup, Restorative Vegetable 36
Moroccan Couscous 46
Moroccan Spice Blend 107
Mushrooms:
  Chicken Cacciatore 76
  Mushroom Ragout 56
  Restorative Vegetable Miso Soup 36
Mussels, Linguine & 72

N
New England Lobster Boil 70

O
Oats:
  Chef Art's Smart Start Blueberry
    Oatmeal 27
  Chewy Almond Butter & Oatmeal Bars 95
  Overnight Banana-Pecan Oatmeal 23
  Peach & Blueberry Crisp 92
  Peanut Butter Cup Cookie 96
Ooey Gooey Mocha Chocolate Cake 87
Oranges:
  Moroccan Couscous 46
  Orange Vinaigrette 103
  Pickled Beet & Orange Salad To-Go 32
  Overnight Banana-Pecan Oatmeal 23

P
Pantry:
  Caramelized Onions 100
  Cooked Pickled Beets 99
5-Minute Baby Food
  Beet Puree 109
  Pea Puree 109
  Sweet Potato Puree 109
5-Minute Marinades
  Asian Marinade 105
  Dijon Mustard Chicken Marinade 105
  Tandoori Chicken Marinade 105
Green Goddess Dressing 101
Mediterranean Salad Dressing 102
Orange Vinaigrette 103
Smith Family Garden Pickles 98
2-Minute Spice Blends
  Indian Spice Blend 107
  Mediterranean Herb Blend 107
  Moroccan Spice Blend 107
Peach & Blueberry Crisp 92
Peanut Butter Cup Cookie 96
Pears:
  Cauliflower, Leek, & Fennel Soup 37
  Turkey Sausage Stuffed Pears 20
Peas:
  Mediterranean Salad to-Go 35
  Pea Puree 109
  Pea & Summer Squash Soup 41
Pecan Oatmeal, Overnight Banana 23
Pickled Beet & Orange Salad To-Go 32
Pickles, Smith Family Garden 98
Pine Nuts:
  Mediterranean Salad to-Go 35
Polenta:
  Creamy Polenta 55

Index

Meatballs with Creamy Polenta & Red Sauce 75
Pomegranate & Chia Seed Topping, Chocolate Pudding with 88

Popcorn:
Mexican-Spiced Chocolate 94
Rosemary & Thyme Caramel Popcorn 83

Pork:
Meatballs with Creamy Polenta & Red Sauce 75

Potatoes: See also Sweet Potatoes
Fingerling Potatoes 58
New England Lobster Boil 70
Traditional Southern Ham Hash 13

Q

Quinoa:
Farmhouse Chopped Salad To-Go 31

R

Ragout, Mushroom 56

Raspberries:
Chocolate Pudding with Pomegranate & Chia Seed Topping 88
Restorative Vegetable Miso Soup 36
Rice Bowls, Asian 61
Rosemary & Thyme Caramel Popcorn 83

S

Salad Dressings:
Green Goddess Dressing 101
Mediterranean Salad Dressing 102
Orange Vinaigrette 103

Salads:
Farmhouse Chopped Salad To-Go 31
Mediterranean Salad to-Go 35
Pickled Beet & Orange Salad To-Go 32
Salmon & Kale 65

Salsa:
Huevos Rancheros 28
Salsa Verde Shrimp Tacos 66

Sausage:
Sausage & Peppers 73
Turkey Sausage Stuffed Pears 20

Seafood:
Halibut with Spinach & Tomatoes 62
Linguine & Mussels 72
Low-Country Shrimp & Grits 69
New England Lobster Boil 70
Salmon & Kale 65
Salsa Verde Shrimp Tacos 66

Sesame:
Asian Rice Bowls 61

Shrimp:
Low-Country Shrimp & Grits 69
Salsa Verde Shrimp Tacos 66

Side Dishes:
Braised Kale with Lardons 49
Broccoli with Thai Peanut Sauce 51
Chef Art's Garlicky Mashed Cauliflower 53
Creamy Polenta 55
Fingerling Potatoes 58
Ginger-Soy Brussels Sprouts 48
Green Beans Almondine 50
Moroccan Couscous 46
Mushroom Ragout 56
Sweet Potatoes with Maple Syrup, Marshmallows & Rosemary 57
Tabbouleh 45
Warm Summer Squash with Feta Cheese 52
Smith Family Garden Pickles 98

Soups:
Cauliflower, Leek, & Fennel Soup 37
Creamy Butternut Squash & Apple Soup 39
Pea & Summer Squash Soup 41
Restorative Vegetable Miso Soup 36
Turkey Chili 42
Tuscan Tomato Soup 40

Spice Blends: See 2-Minute Spice Blends

Spinach:
Caramelized Onion, Spinach & Gruyere Strata 19
Farmhouse Chopped Salad To-Go 31
Halibut with Spinach & Tomatoes 62
Pea & Summer Squash Soup 41
Restorative Vegetable Miso Soup 36
Spinach Dip 80

Squash:
Creamy Butternut Squash & Apple Soup 39
Pea & Summer Squash Soup 41
Restorative Vegetable Miso Soup 36
Warm Summer Squash with Feta Cheese 52

Sunflower Seeds:
Farmhouse Chopped Salad To-Go 31

Sweet Potatoes:
Sweet Potatoes with Maple Syrup, Marshmallows & Rosemary 57
Sweet Potato Puree 109

T

Tabbouleh 45
Tacos, Salsa Verde Shrimp 66

Tandoori Chicken Marinade 105

Tomatoes:
Chicken Cacciatore 76
Halibut with Spinach & Tomatoes 62
Meatballs with Creamy Polenta & Red Sauce 75
Mediterranean Poached Egg 16
Sausage & Peppers 73
Tabbouleh 45
Turkey Chili 42
Tuscan Tomato Soup 40
Traditional Southern Ham Hash 13

Turkey:
Turkey Chili 42
Turkey Sausage Stuffed Pears 20
Tuscan Tomato Soup 40

2-Minute Spice Blends:
Indian Spice Blend 107
Mediterranean Herb Blend 107
Moroccan Spice Blend 107

V

Vegetables: See also Side Dishes and specific vegetable
Restorative Vegetable Miso Soup 36
Smith Family Garden Pickles 98
Spinach Dip 80
Veggies Cooking Chart 9

W

Walnuts:
Chef Art's Smart Start Blueberry Oatmeal 27
Pickled Beet & Orange Salad To-Go 32
Warm Brie with Fig Preserves & Almonds 84
Warm Summer Squash with Feta Cheese 52
Weeknight Chicken Breast 78
What is Smartbowl? 6
Whole "Roasted" Garlic 81

Y

Yogurt:
Chef Art's Garlicky Mashed Cauliflower 53
Green Goddess Dressing 101
Ooey Gooey Mocha Chocolate Cake 87
Pea & Summer Squash Soup 41
Turkey Chili 42

Z

Zucchini:
Warm Summer Squash with Feta Cheese 52